AF429267

Noah & The Pre-Flood World

Dr. David Tee

Published by Dr. David Tee, 2024.

While every precaution has been taken in the preparation of this book, the publisher assumes no responsibility for errors or omissions, or for damages resulting from the use of the information contained herein.

NOAH & THE PRE-FLOOD WORLD

First edition. September 16, 2024.

Copyright © 2024 Dr. David Tee.

ISBN: 979-8227992468

Written by Dr. David Tee.

Table of Contents

Dr. David Tee

Cover image by Pexels

All rights reserved

Copyrighted 2024

Introduction

The pre-flood world enigma

The Merriam-Webster Dictionary defines the term enigma as "something hard to understand or explain (source). That is exactly how it is with the pre-flood world that Noah lived in.

However, unlike other enigmas, we have some very good clues as to what the pre-flood world was comprised of and how the people lived. This book explores this mysterious world by following the clues found in the Bible and research areas.

We cannot provide a very clear picture as we are not given too many details about this civilization. But we do get a glimpse through the lifestyles of the population that turned from God and lived a complete life of sin.

What we do know clearly about the pre-flood world is that they were like the people Jude describes in his short epistle. Jude says in verse 11 "11 Woe to them! For they have gone the way of Cain".

Then in verse 15 "to execute judgment upon all, and to convict all the ungodly of all their ungodly deeds which they have done in an ungodly way, and of all the harsh things which ungodly sinners have spoken against Him."

This is what we know was the end result of the pre-flood world civilization. Their punishment was left to the post-flood world as a warning to all those who chose the path of Cain. As Peter said in his second epistle:

"5 and did not spare the ancient world, but protected Noah, a preacher of righteousness, with seven others, when He brought a flood upon the world of the ungodly; 6 and if He condemned the cities of Sodom and Gomorrah to destruction by reducing them to ashes, having made them an example of what is coming for the ungodly..."

But what was the pre-flood world really like? How did they live? What did they believe? What technology was available to them? What brought them to the point where God had enough and said it was time for a change?

These are the topics that are discussed in the following pages. The clues that we have point to an interesting lifestyle that would shock some people. Not for the cruelty or the sensationalism that took place during those early years of Earth's history.

Rather, readers will be shocked that the clues point to a lifestyle that is very similar to the one taking place today. If they read the following pages, they should see how close the two worlds are in behavior, thought, word, and desires.

It seems that the post-flood world has ignored the warnings of the Flood and the destruction of Sodom and Gomorrah and has decided to live like their pre-flood world counterparts.

While the post-flood world will not get down to one righteous man before God acts, the fact that more than a few billion people will be lost is tragic and a sad affair.

The fact that evil has been so successful in deceiving not just one world's population but a large majority of a second should cause believers to pause and re-examine their lives.

As Solomon said in Ecclesiastes 1 "9 What has been, it is what will be,

And what has been done, it is what will be done. So there is nothing new under the sun. 10 Is there anything of which one might say,

"See this, it is new"? It has already existed for ages Which were before us.

11 There is no remembrance of the earlier things..."

That last line is prophetic as today's population do not remember what took place in the pre-flood world. Nor do they seem to care that they are doing the exact same things that brought that first civilization to destruction.

The enigma of the pre-flood world is that we only get an idea of what they did that caused God to start over. We do not see their building plans, their geography, their religious beliefs, or their daily lives.

We can only assume that they went to school and had similar academic institutions as we have today, that they worked 6 days a week, and so on. We know that they had romance as the Bible tells us that they were given in marriage and married (Luke 17: 26-27).

We know of their construction achievements but only in passing. The mysterious structures of today were built by them and destroyed in the flood. We do not know everything they built and if they needed or used prisons like the ones used throughout the post-flood world.

However, we also know that just about everything that existed in that era was destroyed so we know nothing about it except for the few clues that still exist. The following pages go through those few clues to shed some light on how the pre-flood population lived.

It covers their religious beliefs, their sins, and the possible technological tools and advancements they may have had. Also, it shows that the pre-flood world was not without high culture as music was part of their lives.

In addition to those topics, the following pages look at the possible geography of the pre-flood world, including the status of Antarctica. It stands to reason that ice-covered continent may not have been ice-covered despite what scientists claim today.

Another topic this book will delve into will be the pre-flood world's diet. It also suggests that the inhabitants of that era did not stick to God's diet and their rebellion including violating it.

Not to be left out, the book discusses the scientific ideas of super continents and mass extinctions. Science thinks that multiple mass extinctions were going back almost 500 million years.

Yet, it is hard to see how they can differentiate between them and prove which animals died when. Science also likes to talk about how the super continents roamed the earth but that is a theory based on the looks of the current continents.

It is highly doubtful that the pre-flood world looked very much different than the post-flood world looks like today, with a couple of exceptions. The possibility of lost continents may have been part of the pre-flood world.

We just can never be sure although the clues point to expanded land masses and smaller oceans. The problem for the scientists is that they will never be able to verify their claims while the evidence for Noah's flood keeps piling up to such an extent that readers will find it hard to ignore anymore.

In the author's other book on the biblical flood, Noah's Flood Did Take Place, the evidence for the flood is far greater and verifiable than what the scientists can do for their theories on the ancient world.

The evidence for Noah;'s flood is there and readers should not ignore it like they do the warnings God has left. It is the only biblical event that has more than enough evidence proving it is historical and true.

Take a look at how the pre-flood world lived and thought. Then compare it to today's world to get an idea of what is coming soon. We may not have too many years left on this planet and we still have a lot of work to do before Christ returns.

That is what this book is all about. The contents serve not only as a warning but as a reminder to believers to get their lives in order and live their lives in accordance to God's word.

Believers do not have much time left to make an impact for Jesus and there are a lot of people still in need of a savior. Time to roll up our sleeves and get to work.

DR. DAVID TEE

Image by Imaresz

Noah & the Pre-Flood World

Answering the Critics

The author of the paper 'The Impossible Voyage of Noah's Ark' has this to say in his concluding remarks:

"Our study of the epic of Noah has two results: we have shown beyond any reasonable question that such a voyage never took place and could not possibly have ever occurred. We have demonstrated that those who accept this tale are using not knowledge but faith—the faith of that irrational variety expressed in the old quip as "believing something that you know isn't true." (Moore, 1983)

However, he has done no such thing. In fact, he has violated many logical fallacies in his effort. There is not space or time enough to address every single point he makes and show why they are wrong.

Suffice it to say that his point of view comes from a pre-drawn conclusion/assumption, that evolution is true and the Bible is false. There is no attempt at objectivity nor consideration that he may be in error.

Image by Fabien

The definition of logical fallacies

It is important to understand what logical fallacies are to see where the critic of the biblical account went wrong-

"Logical fallacies are bogus modes of reasoning that can appear legitimate but in fact violate accepted rules of inference. Logical fallacies can be tricky. By masquerading as legitimate arguments, they can fool us into thinking that they are legitimate. But closer inspection reveals the critical flaw at the heart of any given logical fallacy. Such flaws are not always easily detected, especially in the heat of debate." (Carlson, 2024)

Keep in mind that the list and definition for and of logical fallacies are created by unbelievers. They may not be accurate in scope and usually applied at times when the unbelieving critic needs to avoid the truth.

The violated logical fallacies

We cannot deal with all of the violations the critic of Noah's Flood committed. In this section, only a few will be addressed. All definitions will be taken from an article written by K. Hesterberg in 2022:

#1. The Personal Incredulity Fallacy - "If you have difficulty understanding how or why something is true, that doesn't automatically mean the thing in question is false. A personal or collective lack of understanding isn't enough to render a claim invalid"

The author of the paper in question has great difficulty in understanding how or why something is true. He accepts evolution and merely applies his personal opinion at the end of the paper without presenting any hard evidence as to why his view is correct.

#2. The Burden of Proof Fallacy- "If a person claims that X is true, it is their responsibility to provide evidence in support of that assertion. It is invalid to claim that X is true until someone else can prove that X is not true. Similarly, it is also invalid to claim that X is true because it's impossible to prove that X is false."

The author presents a lot of referenced claims, yet he says his 'evidence' proves the Bible is not true, even though he cannot prove the validity of his claims.

He says he is correct and no one can prove him wrong. His problem is that his referenced 'evidence' only works in the post-flood world as he has no idea of the knowledge and expertise of Noah and his family.

#3. The Texas Sharpshooter Fallacy- "This fallacy gets its colorful name from an anecdote about a Texan who fires his gun at a barn wall, and then proceeds to paint a target around the closest cluster of bullet holes. He then points at the bullet-riddled target as evidence of his expert marksmanship.

Speakers who rely on the Texas sharpshooter fallacy tend to cherry-pick data clusters based on a predetermined conclusion."

The author has done this with every argument he makes against the biblical account. He writes from a pre-determined point of view and cherry-picks the data he will target.

He has no basis to make these arguments as too much information is missing from the biblical account.

#4. The Hasty Generalization Fallacy- "This fallacy occurs when someone draws expansive conclusions based on inadequate or insufficient evidence. In other words, they jump to conclusions about the validity of a proposition with some — but not enough — evidence to back it up, and overlook potential counterarguments"

This is one of the major violations that the author has made in his paper. He has drawn his conclusions about Noah, his family, and what they know then built his strawman arguments (another fallacy violated) against those assumptions.

His own paper and argument fail because of these violations and because the arguments he makes are based on nothing but what he expects to be included in the Bible.

#5. The Strawman Fallacy- This fallacy occurs when your opponent over-simplifies or misrepresents your argument (i.e., setting up a "straw man") to make it easier to attack or refute. Instead of fully addressing your actual argument, speakers relying on this fallacy present a superficially similar — but ultimately not equal — version of your real stance, helping them create the illusion of easily defeating you."

This violation is found in the critic's section on animals. He uses the word 'species' not 'kinds' thus changing the target of his criticism. The Bible does not say 'species', it says 'kind'.

This difference changes the number of animals' dynamic. He is saying over 1,000,000 animals were on the ark when there may be as little as 500. As science has proven, 'kinds' develop a variety of 'species' not vice versa.

Species cannot develop kinds.

The other arguments failures

The author of that paper not only violates the logical fallacies but he bases his point of view on 3 other types of arguments.

#1. The argument from silence- he does not know what Noah and his family did during the building of the ark but has built arguments based on the fact the Bible does not mention Noah's and his family's construction or veterinarian skills, to name just two.

He has to verify the fact that Noah and his family were incapable in all areas he mentions but has failed to produce one shred of evidence proving he is correct. The Bible is about God, his commands, etc., and what he did in our history.

The Bible is not about Noah and his abilities. There is going to be a lot of missing information we can never get back which would prove the critic is misleading his readers and would provide the information he is looking for.

#2. The argument from the assumption- since the critic does not know anything about Noah and his family, he assumes that they do not have the capability to perform all the tasks involved in the construction and stay in the ark.

He also assumes and criticizes those Christians who say Noah and his family hired workers to help them. We do not know what Noah and his family did during the construction phase.

They may have paid help to ensure solid construction but we will never know. it is also a possibility that God provided them step-by-step instructions as they went.

Every one of his arguments is based solidly on silence and assumption. But there is a third argument error the critic made. One example is found later in the paper where it reads:

"Finally one day, a typically gargantuan wave sent the ark crashing into the cliffs on Mt. Ararat, and the long voyage was through. But Noah's luck was still running badly, for he had gone from the frying pan into the fire, landing on an active volcano."

The critic needs to prove that a gigantic wave was responsible for the ark's final resting place. Plus, he changes the Bible and says it landed on a volcano called Mt. Ararat.

The Bible simple says 'the mountains of Ararat in a location that was safe and far from any volcanic activity.

#3. The argument of omission- He omits the fact that God has the power and knowledge to guide the construction of the ark. Plus, he also can take care of the wood so it would not rot during that period.

On top of that, he has the knowledge and skills, not to mention the power, to take care of the animals. Since God gave Noah the direction to build the ark, understandably, he would ensure everything was perfect so the inhabitants of the ark were safe and well-cared for.

You cannot leave God out of the picture after he instituted the project. God had his hand on the ark and would not let anything happen to it or its inhabitants.

Yes, miracles were a part of the flood. That is to be expected when God is a part of the situation.

Conclusion

The critics, not just this one, create fanciful tales about the Biblical account. In making their opposition known to Christians and others, they tend, like this critic, to violate their own argumentative standards.

Throughout that paper, the critic created one false tale after another, then used those false tales to criticize the Bible. If God included all the information unbelievers or critics want to see in the Bible, then the book would be so thick, boring, and hard to understand that no one would read it.

In that situation, no one would get the message or warning God is leaving for the post-flood population. That warning is found in 2 Peter 2:5ff which states that the flood and Sodom & Gomorrah were left as warnings to those who refuse to repent of their sinful ways and accept Christ as their savior.

God is saying, destruction will come to all who follow the pre-flood world's example. The Bible is not about how the ark was built or how Noah and his family were to look after the animals, etc.

The Bible reveals what needs to be done to be saved from destruction and punishment. Focusing on information that can never be recovered is one way to distract oneself from the truth.

The truth is one needs to accept Christ as their savior to avoid what took place at Noah's flood.

Work Cited

Carlson, B., (2024), "30 Common Logical Fallacies—A Study Starter", Academic Influence, Retrieved from https://academicinfluence.com/inflection/study-guides/logical-fallacies#strawman

Hestererberg, K., (2022), "16 Common Logical Fallacies and How to Spot Them" Hub Spot, retrieved from https://blog.hubspot.com/marketing/common-logical-fallacies

Moore, R., (1983), 'The Impossible Voyage of Noah's Ark', National Center for Science Education, Creation/Evolution Journal, Volume 4 No. 1 Winter

1983, Retrieved from https://ncse.ngo/impossible-voyage-noahs-ark#Conclusion

Noah and Creation

How did the creation account get to Moses?

This is an important question. Fortunately, it does have an answer but not one that many people would expect or accept. Too many people are focused on the Babylonian captivity and say the biblical writers copied from the Babylonian creation account, the Enuma Elish.

That is not even a possibility as Kenneth Kitchen wrote:

"The common assumption that the Hebrew account is simply a purged and simplified version of the Babylonian legend . . . is fallacious on methodological grounds.

In the Ancient Near East, the rule is that simple accounts or traditions may give rise (by accretion and embellishment) to elaborate legends, but not vice versa. In the Ancient Orient, legends were not simplified or turned into pseudo-history (historicized) as has been assumed for early Genesis." (1)

There is no real explanation as to how the Babylonians or the over 100 other ancient societies received their creation stories if Moses or the biblical writers copied from the Babylonians.

Then, since Moses was never in contact with the Babylonians, how did he write a creation account?

Where would he get his information?

Some scholars would say that he was taught it while being raised by the Pharaoh's daughter. The Egyptians do have a creation account (2) but it is highly unlikely that Moses would reject what his mother taught him in favor of such an embellished and fanciful tale the Egyptians had concocted (3).

Given Mr. Kitchen's scholarly words, it is doubtful that Moses would take that embellished and weird creation account and turn it into something simple, coherent, logical, and orderly. The details in the Egyptian account would not provide Moses with enough inspiration or details for him to write what is found in Genesis 1 or 2.

Image byJohnReimer

Chronology is the key

While older manuscripts provide a creation story, their age does not indicate that they were the first ones written. These manuscripts and their discovery do not indicate that Moses or any other biblical writer copied from them.

There is no historical connection to any of the other extant accounts, save for the Egyptian one, but where did the Egyptians and ancient civilizations get their accounts from in the first place?

To get this information, we have to go back to the time before the flood. Noah and his family pre-date every ancient creation account and post-flood people. He was a direct descendant of Seth whose son influenced people to call on the name of the Lord.

Through this act, God was able to preserve what he did. Adam told his children, they told their children and eventually, the account reached Noah. Since Noah was a righteous man, he would not change any of the creation details.

Instead, he would accept them and teach them to his children and possibly their wives (if they had not already heard of how life began). We cannot be certain what the wives believed because we know nothing about them except they were not daughters of Noah).

But their almost year-long stay on the ark would expose them to the truth, thus they would have the same story as Noah and his wife had. This is important because, after the flood, they taught their descendants the truth.

This would be true of Shem and Japheth but we cannot be sure what Ham and his wife taught their children. Shem was the ancestor of Abraham, which gives us a clue as to why he was selected by God.

He would have heard the accounts from his ancestors, possibly from Shem himself, as Shem lived 500 years after the flood. Abraham was born roughly 290 years after the flood.

This puts him right in the middle of Shem's long after flood life. Thus, we have an eyewitness that would have told the truth for 5 centuries impacting any descendants' life.

The story of creation would have been passed down from Adam to all of his children who eventually passed it down to Noah who passed it to his children, who passed it on to their descendants after the flood.

Abraham would have passed it down to Isaac who would have told Jacob and on it goes till it finally reaches Moses' ears. Moses did not have to write before the other ancient flood accounts to be the first and the original creation record.

The Enuma Elish is dated between 1200 and 2000 BC (4) which means it could easily have been recorded long after Moses wrote Genesis. How the Babylonians received the account can be explained in several ways.

One is that they were exposed to the account when they took the Israelites captive. This scenario would mean that the dating for the Enuma Elish is off. Or, the future Babylonians heard the account from Noah and his sons or wives and when the world was divided at Babel.

They simply recorded their own version as their religious and other beliefs strayed from God and the truth. We know that they strayed as the Babylonians worshiped a variety of false gods.

Those are just two reasonable explanations and there may be more.

Copying is not a factor

Many scholars have not given up on the idea that the biblical writers copied from the Babylonians during their Babylonian exile. They hold to this position despite two key factors.

The first factor is that the Israelites never enjoyed a reputation for being copyists of other people's religious and historical documents. There was no need for them to copy as they already knew their history.

It had been taught to them for generations through copies of the Pentateuch and other books of the Old Testament. The stories of Babylon would seem like myths and fairy tales to them even during the exile.

The second factor is that the Old Babylonians were known to be copyists and had a rich reputation for copying everything they could get their hands on (5). How the Babylonians got their creation account could easily be explained by the two options above or this third option that they copied from other nations they did have contact with.

That is not far-fetched as an individual Babylonian could easily be told the story by a citizen of those nations, then asked to see the record, and finally be inspired to write their own version of events according to their religious beliefs.

The question, why would the Israelites incorporate their enemy's religious works into their own holy works has never been satisfactorily explained by any scholars. There is no evidence supporting that idea.

It wouldn't make sense as the people of Israel would have their copies of the Old Testament long before and when they went into exile. They would know the stories would be false and most likely demand that they be removed from their scriptures.

Even though important other people's religious content into one's alternative religious holy books has been known to take place; those actions have generally been alternative religious leaders importing biblical content into their writings not vice versa.

There is evidence for this as the Book of Mormon and the Qur'an both were written long after the biblical content was written, published, and well-known. Those are just two holy books that borrowed greatly from the Bible.

Any accusations that the New Testament writers borrowed from the many secret religions have been successfully refuted. Physical evidence backs up the refutation as the writings of the secret religions containing biblical information were written long after the New Testament books were written, published, and distributed (6).

The physical evidence proves the chronology and shows how Moses received the correct account of creation. But even if it did not happen that way, Moses had ample time in Midian and on Mount Sinai to get the correct information from God.

Scholars have a different idea

One of the problems Christians have to deal with is the conclusions of the scholars. These educated men and women have different ideas about how the Bible received the creation account.

They place the dating to a period long after Moses had died and roughly around the time of the Babylonian exile. They conclude that:

"The latest books of the Hebrew Bible, such as Esther and Ezra-Nehemiah, describe events from the fifth century B.C.E. and would have been written afterward—meaning that the very earliest the Hebrew Bible could have been compiled in its entirety is the fifth century B.C.E., with some scholars suggesting much later dates...There are two main reasons why many scholars think reading and writing were not prevalent in ancient Israel and Judah until the eighth century B.C.E." (7)

However, there is no evidence supporting this or any scholars' argument that the Old Testament was written so long after Moses lived. We know that writing existed with the people of Israel long before Israel became an independent nation.

Scholars and unbelievers just do not accept that physical evidence but fail to produce any physical evidence for their arguments.

Some additional words

It is easy to see if one follows the evidence, that the original creation story is the one found in the Bible. There are no rational, logical, or even reasonable explanations for why it exists at all unless it is true and the original.

It is reasonable, logical, and rational to accept the fact that the other ancient nations' creation accounts could only come from what their ancestors were taught prior to Babel.

The differences come from the influence of those ancient nations' new religious and other beliefs as they strayed further from God. The choice of what to believe is left up to the reader and all people.

One can accept the facts as laid out above or follow the ancient unbelievers into wild and fancy myths and legends that only took place in their imaginations.

Myths and legends are often based on real events and the many creation and flood accounts prove this is true.

Works Cited

#1. (Kenneth Kitchen, Ancient Orient and the Old Testament, Chicago; InterVarsity Press, 1966, p. 89). Retrieved from https://www.blueletterbible.org/faq/don_stewart/don_stewart_645.cfm

#2. History Collection, (2019) "16 Incredible Ancient Creation Stories from Around the World", #14 Retrieved from https://historycollection.com/16-incredible-ancient-creation-stories-from-around-the-world/

#3. Exodus 2

#4. Mark, J.J., (2018), "Enuma Elish - The Babylonian Epic of Creation", World History Encyclopedia, Retrieved from https://www.worldhistory.org/article/225/enuma-elish—-the-babylonian-epic-of-creation—-fu/

#5. Chavalas, M.W & Younger, K.L., ed., (2002), "Mesopotamia and the Bible: Comparative Explorations", Baker Books, approx. Pg. 243.

#6. Strobel, L., (2007), "In defense of Jesus", Zondervan, Chapter 4, pg. 165ff

#7. BAS Staff, (2023), "When Was the Bible Written?", Biblical Archaeology Society- Bible HistoryDaily, Retrieved from https://www.biblicalarchaeology.org/daily/ancient-cultures/ancient-israel/when-was-the-bible-written/

Noah & the pre-Flood Culture

Image by Sippakorn Yamkasikorn

Introduction

The Bible does not talk that much about the pre-flood world. It is our only source about that original civilization. Talking about the pre-flood world is not the focus of the Bible.

Instead, it provides enough information to see how God interacted with that population and show us a little more about who God is. If it provided any more details, not only would the Bible become boring, and probably too thick to encourage anyone to read it.

However, the Bible does provide clues as to the culture of that time and a glimpse of how the people lived. Archaeology can fill in some of the blanks but only if people believe that the pre-flood world existed (which it did).

Noah lived in the last years of this culture which is why we get a glimpse of what life was like in that era.

They were human (Gen. 1 -6)

This is one of the most important aspects of this culture. Even the giants were humans and not some celestial/terrestrial mix. They had the same needs as post-flood humans and required food, shelter, and employment, to name a few necessities.

Science may claim that other sub-human species were alive at the time and for millions of years, yet science cannot verify one claim they make about the early humanoids. In other words, those human variations did not exist. Only humans did.

Because they were humans, they needed to grow food, raise livestock, and build structures for their housing, employment needs as well as for their recreational needs, and so on.

We find remnants of those buildings throughout the world and under the ocean. Because they were human, those villages, cities, and other residences were built near fresh water sources just like the modern population builds their homes, etc.

They were made in God's image (Gen. 1:26)

Being made in God's image does not mean that they were spirits who could live anywhere. One definition of the word 'image' is "A representation or similitude of any person or thing (1).

This means that humans were not made exactly like God but held key characteristics that God has. Humans were made to think, have emotions, intelligence, and similar characteristics we find n God.

Instead of being given a celestial body, God gave them a human form that was perfect for the environment he had created for humans. The pre-flood humans could do everything that the post-flood population could do, even make choices.

The pre-flood world people were just like us in every way down to having preferences for food, romantic relationships, and much more.

They had a knowledge of God (Gen. 3 &4)

To some people, the pre-flood world may seem like the population were ignorant knuckle draggers whose only thoughts were about survival and nothing else.

This is far from the truth. As we see by these two chapters, Adam & Eve both knew about and knew God. When they ate the fruit they were not supposed to eat, they became afraid of God when he came to be with them in the Garden of Eden.

The couple had a relationship with God but the Bible does not go into details about that relationship. Instead, the Bible focuses on what happens when God's creation disobeys him.

Even when cast out of the Garden, the knowledge of God did not disappear. In chapter 4 we read where Cain and Abel brought sacrifices to God. We can presume that Adam and Eve taught not just Cain and Abel about God but their other children also got this lesson.

The knowledge of God was evident at the time when Seth was born as the end of Chapter 4 tells everyone that at that birth, the people alive at the time started to call upon the name of the Lord.

This knowledge of God continues into the 5th chapter as we read two important details. One, Enoch walked with God & two, Noah was a righteous man.

This is just like today where people have a knowledge of God or walk with him. Plus they have the choice to be righteous as well.

They had a choice

It is not sure exactly when the pre-flood world started down the slippery slope to destruction but most likely it began slowly with Cain's sin. How big an influence Cain's sin had over the pre-flood world and how quickly they got to the point where God was sorry he made man, is not known.

What is known is that the pre-flood world had a choice to walk a sinful route or walk the righteous path. Everyone knows that eventually, almost all people choose the sinful path.

Details are scant on when this slide really took hold over the pre-flood culture, but those details are not important. What is important is that 99.999% of the population choose the wrong route and constantly thought of evil all day long (Gen. 6)

Only Noah and his family remained on the righteous path and avoided the destruction that was to come.

The pre-flood culture had music & industry (Gen 4)

It may surprise some people that the pre-flood culture was much like the post-flood one. The people did not spend their time just lurking in caves, painting the walls, or waiting for animals to come by to get food.

There was more to that culture than what scientists and anthropologists claim took place in our past. Three descendants of Cain were given the honor of being 'the father of'. Thus many of the post-flood music and other industries owe their existence to these three men.

" 20 Adah gave birth to Jabal; he was the father of those who live in tents and have livestock. 21 His brother's name was Jubal; he was the father of all those who play the lyre and flute. 22 As for Zillah, she also gave birth to Tubal-Cain, the forger of all implements of bronze and iron...”(Gen 4).

Cattle, sheep, and other livestock ranching, as well as the nomadic life, musicians, and metal work, were all a part of the pre-flood world. What music and other forms of entertainment they created is not known as it was all destroyed in the flood.

But the industries were carried forward. While they may not have had TV shows and movies to watch, they most certainly had entertainment at different levels. Solomon made that clear in Ecclesiastes 1 when he wrote that nothing was new under the sun.

What took and takes place in the post-flood world, was already thought of and took place in the pre-flood culture. Just the forms may be different due to technological discoveries but we cannot even be sure of that as the pre-flood world was technologically advanced.

There were construction and manufacturing jobs as well as businesses related to those two industries. We see this in the myriad of mysterious structures found around the world. There is no other explanation for these structures to have existed and destroyed.

Archaeologists may say that certain early primitive cultures built these complicated structures, stone heads, and similar mysteries but those cultures did not have the tools to construct these buildings.

Nor do the archaeologists have a valid explanation as to why the knowledge of this construction disappeared. It is unlikely for the knowledge to completely disappear through normal life as we know it.

The modern age is rife with industrial espionage which tells us that other countries desire the knowledge and technological developments. Then use that knowledge for their own purposes.

No one destroys valuable data and lets it be lost for millennia. The only explanation for this mysterious technological developments and construction disappearance is the flood.

Image by Yolanda Jost

They lived normal human lives (MT 24)

Despite what the beginning of Genesis 6 has to say, life in the pre-flood world was normal and very much like the post-flood generations. They drank, had fun, ate well, and were married.

Jesus said "For as in those days before the flood they were eating and drinking, marrying and giving in marriage, until the day that Noah entered the ark," (Verse 38).

This gives us a clue into how the pre-flood world lived their lives. They enjoyed food, different beverages, loved, lusted, carried on romantic relationships, gave away their daughters in marriage, and much more.

The culture was exactly like the modern culture is today and has been throughout history. People made choices, lived their lives, and also proved the passage of scripture "Men love darkness rather than light" true. Just like the modern population does.

We can see that the pre-flood world culture was exactly like the post-flood culture. People were deceived, made bad choices, and lived for fun instead of opting to be righteous and avoiding all the sins that led to theirs and the modern world's destruction.

As a side note, with nothing new under the sun, we can say with confidence that the pre-flood world was tolerant of LGBTQ preferences and practices. Among many other abnormalities and perversions.

In both cultures, people prefer sin to what God offers. This is why the Bible talks about the pre-flood world. God is using it as a warning to the post-flood world of what will happen if his creation chooses wrong and lives disobedient lives.

God also uses Sodom & Gomorrah and its destruction as a more modern warning (2 Peter 2: 5 & 6).

Conclusion

Noah's and the pre-flood culture was not unique. It was as human as the modern era and the people of that time, did the exact same things the people of the post-flood eras have done and are doing.

There is no difference between them and us. We should take note of that and heed the warning that God has given in Genesis 6 -9. To avoid what happened to the pre-flood world, the modern-age population must repent of their sins, ask for forgiveness of their sins, and accept Christ as their savior.

The modern societies need to make the choice that the pre-flood world did not make, that is to follow Christ correctly and be holy as he is holy.

Works Cited

#1. Webster, N. (re-published 2006). In Noah Webster's first edition of An American dictionary of the English language. Foundation for American Christian Education.

Image by Galina Afanaseva

Noah & the pre-flood world diet

Food is essential

Some people have remarked that the meat provided by God during the Exodus was an anomaly. Red and other meat was not meant to be part of the regular diet.

To support their case, these people often point to Numbers 11:31. The Israelites craved different food than the manna they received from heaven. They had grown tired of the same food meal after meal.

Then after hearing their complaints, God delivered quail to them. The story did not end well for the Israelites, but this event is not a warning about eating meat.

It had to do more with rejecting God and his provisions for humanity than it had to do with a specific diet. The Israelites were not banned from eating meat. If you check out the diet God gave his people, you will see that a wide assortment of meat is included in what is now called a 'kosher' diet.

The diet of the pre-flood world was different and there may have been a good reason for the restrictions provided.

What the pre-flood world ate

The Bible is very clear on the food Adam and Eve were to eat. In Genesis 2 God permitted Adam to eat of any fruit of any tree except two. But those were not the only sources of food for Adam and the pre-flood world.

We read in Genesis 1 the following words "29 Then God said, "I give you every seed-bearing plant on the face of the whole earth and every tree that has fruit with seed in it. They will be yours for food. 30 And to all the beasts of the earth and all the birds in the sky and all the creatures that move along the ground—everything that has the breath of life in it—I give every green plant for food." And it was so."

Now this gift may have vegans and vegetarians feeling superior to modern-day meat eaters. But there may have been a special reason why God limited their diet to these plants and trees.

He certainly was not saying that animal meat was bad for humans, after all, God made the animal meat and saw that it was good.

Image by Silvia

Why did God limit the diet?

The reasoning is not certain as God does not have to explain himself to his creation. He is God and he acts as he wills. Everyone can rest knowing that God knows what he is doing and the restriction makes sense.

Scholars and archaeologists, scientists, botanists, etc., can theorize as to why God imposed this dietary restriction. The reason may have to do with God's act of creation.

Genesis 1 tells us that he made animals after their kind (v.24-25). It is possible that those words refer to the genetic material he placed in life forms. They may not refer to the concept that God made millions or billions of animals from the start.

He could have but then why would he restrict Adam and Eve to just plants of the Garden? He also could have created millions of people but he started with one pair. In today's mindset, with so many animal species, it is easy for modern Christians and unbelievers to take those words to mean millions of animals were created.

But that may not be the case. Like humans, God may have made only a few animals that would provide the genetic material that would develop into the various species humans have seen throughout history.

Keep in mind that species and kinds are not the same categories. The former group is the result of the mating of the latter group. Genetics has played a large role in creating more species than there are kinds.

Some of those species can mate together and produce fertile offspring. But if those animals from different species mate and are not of the same kind the offspring are often sterile in one gender or the other (source #1).

The many hybrid experiments have proven creation true over the theory of evolution. God said that the animals would produce 'after their kind' (v.20 ff). The problem of sterility is not a mystery to believers who accept Genesis as literally true.

With that said, the reason for the limitation may be that, like humans, the animals needed time to breed. God made just enough kinds, in pairs, like he did humans as his creative process would instill in animals and other life forms all the DNA and other genetic material needed to produce the variety of species that has existed throughout history.

This provides some insight to Day Six of creation, where God caused the animals to pass before Adam and whatever he named them, that would be that kind's name.

Some skeptics have said that for Adam to name all the animals, it would take more years than he lived. But that would only be true if Adam had to name every species. It would not be true if Adam only had to name the original kinds.

This fact greatly reduces the time Adam spent naming the animals. Plus, it would free up a lot of time on Day Six for God to create women from Adam's rib. The problem of time on Day Six is now solved (Answers in Genesis agrees with this point. #2)

Enough animals for food were not available at this time. We are not sure how large Abel's flocks were, we just know that he offered a lamb in sacrifice to God.

As a side note, we are not sure if Abel married and had children at the time of his murder. Thus to speak only of a Seth and Cain genealogical line is presumptuous.

Some insight to the nature of evil

Genesis 6 talks about how evil the world was at the time of the Flood. It is presumptuous to assume that the only evil that was taking place was crime or sexual sins. Those are the main issues that everyone thinks of when they hear the word 'evil.

Yet, God defines evil to include disobedience. With the knowledge that livestock was cultivated not just by Abel, but by Jabal who became the father of all those with livestock (Gen. 3:20) we know that animals were available to eat.

Yet, God's instruction about the diet of the pre-flood world did not change. At least it is not recorded in the Bible if it was. Geneses 3 has this to say in support of this point:

"Cursed is the ground because of you; through painful toil, you will eat food from it all the days of your life." (v.17).

Even when God was angry, he did not permit Adam and his descendants to eat meat. Thus the conclusion that part of the evil performed by the pre-flood world was disobedience to this instruction.

The sinful men saw that animal meat looked good and may have thought that it was a waste to see their meat rot when the animal died. Thus they came up with the idea to kill the animals and eat their meat. This would have been a sin because God had not granted permission for humans to eat meat.

This sin would have been part of the evil that the pre-flood world committed. In chapter 6 of Genesis we read these words: "...They were the heroes of old, men of renown" (v. 4c).

What better way to become a hero and be made famous than to kill many of the large beasts that populated the landscape? Today they are called dinosaurs and when you look at the size of them, it takes a hero to confront and kill them.

When one does it to protect other humans, then their fame grows. However, we cannot limit that portion of the verse to just this one activity. There are other ways for men to become famous and heroes.

The discoveries nameless men made throughout the pre-flood world's history would also achieve the same results. For example, construction methods, the discovery of power, studying the stars, helping farmers grow their groups through different techniques and technology and on it goes.

The pre-flood world was not filled with cave-dwelling knuckle draggers who were afraid of fire. This civilization was filled with intelligent, brave, curious men who sought achievement just like Steve Jobs, Bill Gates, Howard Hughes, and so many other men have done throughout the post-flood world's history.

We can infer that the men of the pre-flood world were of all types of men and sadly, did not stick to a vegan or vegetarian diet. Temptation was alive and well back then as it is now.

The diet did not remain the same

The people who say that the provision of the quail was an anomaly and meat-eating was not part of God's plan for our dietary needs, fail to remember a few key verses in Genesis 9:

"2 The fear and dread of you will fall on all the beasts of the earth, and on all the birds in the sky, on every creature that moves along the ground, and on all the fish in the sea; they are given into your hands. 3 Everything that lives and moves about will be food for you. Just as I gave you the green plants, I now give you everything."

The post-flood world, unlike the pre-flood world, had no dietary restrictions. Everything was free to eat. In some cultures, they have taken that freedom to extremes. In South Korea, they eat silk worms and call beondegi.

In France, they eat frog legs and other interesting crawling creatures, and on it goes. Every culture seems to have some sort of extreme food as a delicacy that was not part of the original diet.

All this means is that the vegan and vegetarian diets are not superior or better for humans than a meat diet. All food is given by God for humans to eat and one should not be so arrogant and call meat eating wrong or sinful.

They are insulting God and his gift to humanity. Eating meat is a gift from God as it clearly states in the last line of those verses immediately above. While people are free to construct their own diets, they should not insult God and call meat-eating bad or unhealthy.

Conclusion

No one is sure of how many animals got off the ark. We know that pairs went in, but it is not known if they were allowed to have offspring during the long months they were being protected from the water.

What is known is that after the flood, Noah, his family, and all humans were allowed to eat meat. We see this permission in the food instructions given by God to the ancient Hebrews.

God included meat in their diet thus humans should include meat in theirs. To criticize God for allowing meat eating is sin and part of the evil that plagues this world.

While we cannot be sure about what exactly the members of the pre-flood world ate, we can infer that meat eating must have been a part of the evil they practiced. According to Genesis 6, all the people thought about was doing evil, and disobedience to the dietary instructions would be sin and a part of evil.

When it comes to modern diets, humans should be careful of what they eat and make sure to include an array of healthy foods, including meat from different animals. We should not be sinning when it comes to our diets.

Works Cited

#1. Manning, AJ, (2023), "Why are hybrid animals sterile?", The Harvard Gazette, https://news.harvard.edu/gazette/story/2023/11/why-are-hybrid-animals-sterile/

#2. Ham, K., (2010), "Did Adam give the animals the names we call them today?", AIG, https://answersingenesis.org/kids/adam-and-eve/did-adam-give-each-of-the-animals-the-names-we-call-them-today

Noah & the Giants

Noah lived at the same time

Genesis 6 starts out talking about the sons of God and the daughters of men. In those few verses, many scholars and other people concluded that the giants were the product of this sinful union.

" 4 The Nephilim were on the earth in those days, and also afterward, when the sons of God came into the daughters of mankind, and they bore children to them. Those were the mighty men who were of old, men of renown."

Yet, the chapter and the rest of scripture do not make any connection between these three groups of people. What we see in the quoted verse are all the believing men creating a union with women they should not have married.

Eventually, these unions corrupted the men of God to the point that all the inhabitants of the pre-flood world thought nothing but evil. We cannot be sure what instructions God gave the people of the pre-flood world or if he outlawed unions between believers and non-believers like he did in the New Testament.

2 Corinthians 6:14 says, " Do not be mismatched with unbelievers; for what do righteousness and lawlessness share together, or what does light have in common with darkness?"

Since God does not change, we must conclude that he had a similar restriction at some point in time before the flood took place. This mismatch matrimony would be one of the evils that they thought of before the end to their civilization came.

But at no time have mismatched unions produced giants. The post-flood world has had countless mismatched unions and no giants appeared. We know today that the size of a person is genetically sourced and does not depend on an unequally yoked marriage.

It must be remembered that giants did not live exclusively in the pre-flood world. Because of genetics we find that giants have lived in the post-flood world- Joshua 12, Deut. 3, Nu. 13, 2 Sam. 21, & Deut. 9.

We are given a glimpse of their personalities in those passages. What we do not know are the personalities of the giants in the pre-flood civilization. However, since the Bible does not explain much about the giants we can conclude that they were like every other citizen of that era.

They too thought of evil all the time. What they did to their fellow humans is not known but it seems that Noah and his family were quite safe even as they built the ark.

With all of the giant fossils found throughout the world and history, we know that Noah did have knowledge and experience with]some species of giants. Exactly how much experience is also unknown. One sea creature measured roughly 30 feet in length sparking debate by scientists (1). Giant human skeletons have also been unearthed in different parts of the world (2).

Credible resources also report on the discovery of giant skeletons (3). These are not the only giant remains that have been found. Evolutionists continue to try to make people believe that the giant dinosaur skeletons died out in a meteorite crash.

Image by Dimitris Vetsikov

Giants are found everywhere

It is not that giants are only found in the biblical realm. Extra-biblical discoveries of giant fossils and humans have been made throughout history proving once and for all that the Nephilim did exist in ancient times.

What encounters Noah and his family had with them is not pertinent to the biblical record so God did not record much about them. However, their presence would explain how such large megalithic stones were put in place so perfectly.

Their combined strength along with whatever tools and equipment were developed by the pre-flood world population would be enough to erect those mysterious structures.

Why do we not see more evidence for giants in the modern world amid all the excavations and construction that take place? The simple and honest answer would be that the pre-flood world did not have a large giant population.

Just like the post-flood world, giant people were rare or scattered due to genetic combinations. There is nothing to indicate that the giants were their own people group or as some modern scientists like to say 'their own race of humans'.

All we know is what the Bible and archaeological discoveries have told us. Giants did exist at one time in the pre-flood world. Their numbers were not important to record as the number of the pre-flood population was not vital and did not need to be recorded in the Bible.

What they did to earn a living could have been anything, including helping Noah and his sons build the ark. Even if the giants did not believe a flood would come that would be large enough to endanger their lives, they still could have worked on the ark.

Unbelievers do not believe Jesus is coming again and they still work for Christians. The belief about the flood would be immaterial as the giants and other pre-flood inhabitants would be looking to provide for their families.

Work is work and taking care of their loved ones would be essential to them. While God gave Noah instructions, those instructions did not exclude Noah from getting construction and boat-building help from the unbelieving world.

Too many unbelievers protest that Noah and his family did not have the skills to build an ark. They may or may not have had boat-building skills. However, their instructions were simply to build it and to use gopher wood, pitch, and make 3 floors, and so on.

Since the pre-flood world was destroyed, details will not be forthcoming about the construction of the ark. It is also possible that the giants helped find the gopher wood, milled it to meet specifications, and delivered it to the construction site.

Then Noah and his sons took it from there. There are a myriad of explanations for how the ark was built. If they used drogue stones to balance the ark, those stones would be large and heavy (4). Help to put them in place would be needed.

These stones are said to be huge and only have one hole near the top. Some people have taken their presence to mean Noah had such stones on the ark. We cannot be sure as we do not know all the details of the ark construction and God did not specify that Noah should use those stones.

Giant skeletons burials are numerous

While the previous references only point to a few burials that some may consider to be suspect, there are far more discoveries than anyone may realize. North American Indian legends speak of giant people walking the earth in their ancestors' time.

These legends are found in the Iroquois, the Osage, the Tuscaroras, the Hurons, the Omahas, and many other North American Indian folklore. But their legends only support the over one thousand accounts of giant skeletons being discovered throughout North America (5).

These discoveries have been documented by a variety of credible sources including scientific reports and the Smithsonian Institute. These documented skeletons range in height from 7 feet to 18 feet in length (ibid).

The 18-foot tall skeleton was found 12 feet under the ground indicating that it had lived and died a very long time ago (Ibid). While there may have been an 18-foot, or a 12-foot tall human on the earth in the pre-flood world, these remains have been rare.

It is not like researchers found 12 and 18-foot skeletons in every one of those thousand+ graves. As to the time of the Indian forefathers, it is hard to tell exactly what era they are referring to.

These stories could have come from their ancestors who lived at Babel and were enthralled by the stories told by Japheth, Shem, and their wives. Again, God did not destroy the memories of these people, he just confused their language so they could not communicate with each other.

What they were told would have traveled with them and used as bedtime or other stories when the original members of the group reproduced. The best that can be said about Noah and the pre-flood giants is that he and his family may have encountered them, worked with them, or they avoided them.

Suffice it to say that the evidence we find today prove that Noah and his sons were well aware of the giants and how evil they had become.

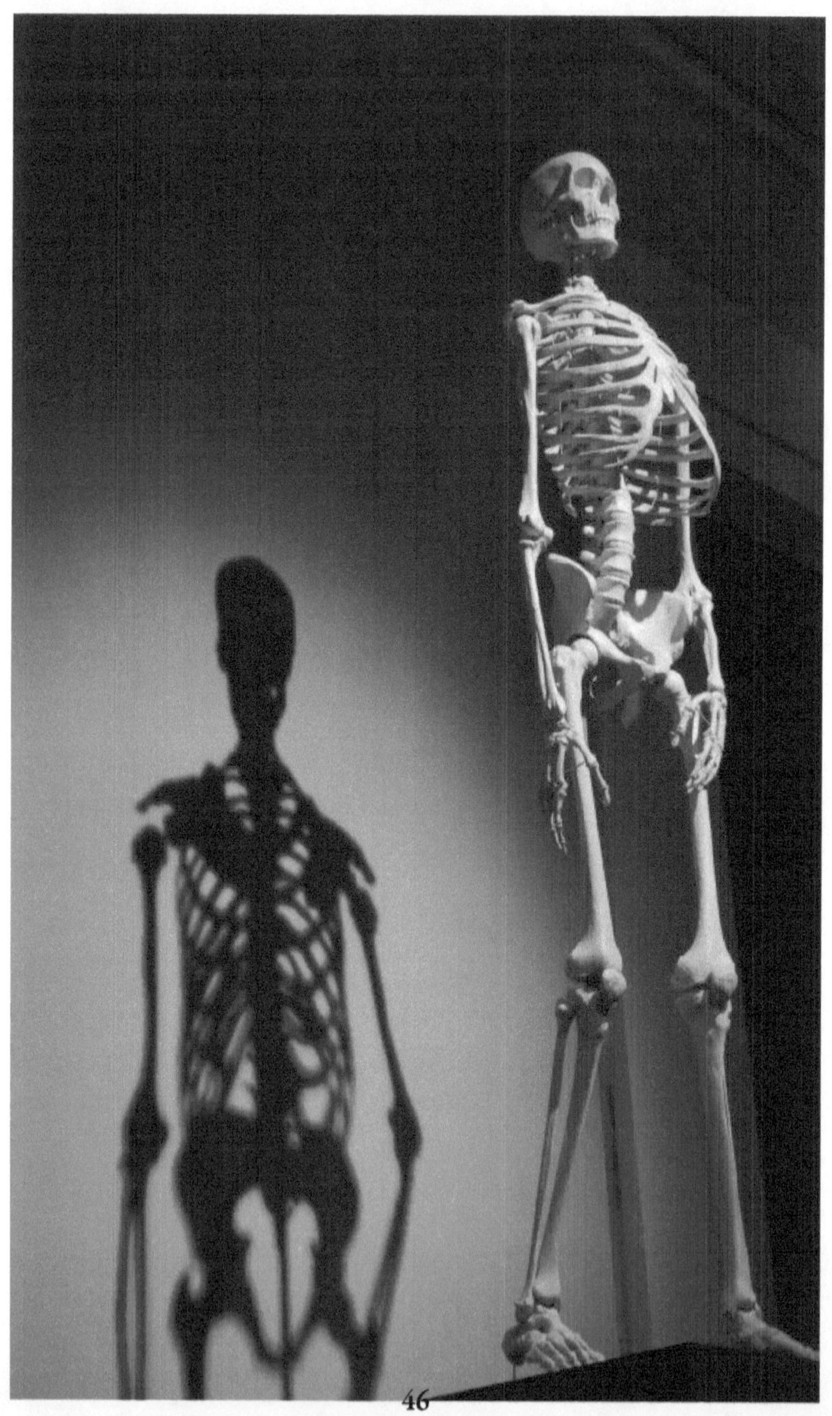

Image by Pixabay

Works Cited

#1. Black, R., (2022), "Giant 'sea monster' fossil is one of the largest of its kind", National Geographic, https://www.nationalgeographic.com/science/article/giant-sea-monster-fossil-is-one-of-the-largest-of-its-kind

#2. farberov, S. (2024), "Scientists still baffled from giant human skeletons up to 10 feet tall decades after initial discovery", NY Post, https://nypost.com/2024/04/04/us-news/mystery-surrounds-peculiar-giant-skeletons-claimed-to-be-found-in-nevada-caves/

#3. AWT, (2020), "The Mystery behind the 18 Giant Skeletons found in the USA", Archaeology World, https://archaeology-world.com/the-mystery-behind-the-18-giant-skeletons-found-in-the-usa/

#4. Renner, R, (2024), "The Ruins of Noah's House", YouTube Video, https://www.youtube.com/watch?v=kXh0uuOxo8c&t=1110s

#5. Newman, H., (2022), "Top Ten Giant Discoveries in North America", Ancient Origins, https://www.ancient-origins.net/unexplained-phenomena/giants-north-america-005196

Noah & the Pre-Flood Geography

Little is known

Without Noah, we probably would not know anything about the pre-flood world. If it wasn't for his righteousness, maybe God would have started all over and re-created the world from scratch.

While the Bible is silent on the pre-flood geography, all it says is that God divided the waters from the land and that is all of the geography lesson we get on this initial geographical landscape.

To the extent the land was divided is also unknown but we can find clues in both literature and science. These clues provide some insight as to how the land looked in Noah's time.

Everyone has theories including talking about super continents that mysteriously divided itself, with the pieces floating to new locations and into the positions we see today.

However, those theories can never be verified. It does not seem logical or rational to have such large land masses capable of holding the weight they do today floating around like some sort of raft.

Were there boats in Noah's time? Most likely there were as Noah and his sons had boat-building knowledge. How big were the boats and how were they used is also anyone's guess. But it does not seem likely that boats were unknown during Noah's time.

The people were to spread out over the land God had created thus boats are a logical answer to the question, how did that population reach around the globe?

What Plato said

Plato's account of the disappearance of Atlantis is well known. It serves no real purpose to repeat it here. Suffice it to say that it is roughly a multi-hand account passed down through generations until Plato recorded it (source 1).

The details of Plato's story can have some foundation in reality. It is not out of the question that an Egyptian priest had the story of the flood destruction. After all, the Egyptians are descendants of the original post-flood one-world civilization who had Noah and his family telling about their experiences.

The ancient Egyptians had their own flood account (2) which would have been derived from the truth of the accounts given by Noah and his family. As time went on, the ancient Egyptians religious beliefs changed and those beliefs influenced someone to alter the story to fit their new beliefs.

Since those ancient accounts were not divinely inspired, it makes sense that the priest either changed the details or was told different details about what he called Atlantis.

Instead of a super continent or several continents being destroyed by a flood, the author of the story the priest told could have simply changed it to an island.

The fact that the civilization on that island was advanced fits perfectly with what we know about the pre-flood world. The knowledge of Noah and his family is preserved in weird yet altered historical accounts that end up being made into myths.

The dating of 9000 BC is probably exaggerated as people will embellish to make their stories sound more interesting and better. There is no reason to accept that date. But the fact that it happened prior to the Egyptian civilization coming into existence is important.

It places the flood at roughly the time chronologically and well before Babel. Geographically, the only clue that is evident is that one island, a rather large one, was destroyed and sunk.

This may fit in with what some scientists claim about our geographical history.

What scientists say

In general, scientists are not believers in the Bible and they do not accept what it says about the Flood. This rejection of the biblical content has led scientists to come up with a lot of theories about how the ancient world once looked like.

They start off with super continents like Pannotia, Gondwana, and Pangea and place these super continents far into the distant past between 175 to 633 million years ago (source-3).

But this seems to be a far-fetched set of theories due to the fact that scientists and science have no special tools and equipment that allows them to see into history (Williams & Hartnett #4).

Nor can they verify their claims. It is very unrealistic to expect any physical evidence to last for 10,000 years let alone for hundreds of millions of years. However, there are some lost continents that science has discovered that may provide some more clues as to what the pre-flood world looked like.

It is impossible to agree with the dates of these lost continents because dating backward is next to impossible. But they do hold some clues and could be used as physical evidence for understanding the pre-flood geography.

These continents, Zealandia, Doggerland, and Mu may not be land masses from myth or fantasy fiction. They may have been parts of the real pre-flood geography as the land masses fit nicely in the vast water expanse we have today.

Mu being an island like Greenland and Australia, could be the source for Plato's Atlantis. The reason these lost continents are selected here is that they are all underneath water.

The evidence from other parts of the world, for example, the Black Sea and the West coast of India tells us that all of the water from the flood did not disappear. God let it remain to change the pre-flood geography into the post-flood land masses we see today.

Another lost continent that could be included in this list is the Louisiade Plateau. It is near Australia also and most of it is beneath the ocean. In fact, roughly 94%+ of each of these lost continents are submerged.

With finding different human and animal remains on Doggerland, this adds to the physical evidence needed to say it was above water before Noah's flood occurred (Ibid).

Judging from the size of these land masses and the amount of water still available, it seems likely that the pre-flood world had boats, especially if they were disobeying God's instructions to eat no meat.

Fishing might have been good during those years. It is hard to say.

Image by Antonius Ntoumas

Did the flood waters create the glaciers?

This is an interesting question since we know that some of the flood waters did not disappear. Maybe some of the waters were trapped and could not exit the planet's surface but that cannot be proven.

Most likely, the planet shifted on its axis creating a different weather system for the post-flood world. Dr. Charles Hapgood determined that the poles did move. However, he determined that it happened more than once (Hapgood, #5).

We doubt anyone could find more than one movement of the earth's axis and one movement seems logical and founded in reality. This movement would have changed the pre-flood beautiful weather into what we have today.

In the areas where glaciers exist and the poles, this pole change brought cooler summers to those regions. With cooler summers, the snow from the previous winters did not melt

Over time, the snows turned to ice and built up to what we have seen throughout history. Thus, the flood waters may have stayed in some regions of the world but not others.

The only reason this can be said is because of the physical evidence found underneath the oceans and seas around the world (Tee #6). This evidence proves that the flood waters remained as there is no other explanation for the submerged remains.

Scientists may speculate about super continents, lost continents, and continents that move and collide with other continents but they cannot verify those speculative ideas. There is no real physical evidence proving those events took place.

Their 'existence' is based merely on the word of the scientists who read their ideas and self-created evidence into what they study.

Conclusion

It is hard to imagine these large continental land masses moving across the ocean until they reach their final resting place. The land masses are far too heavy for that type of movement and there is nothing to say they are not anchored to the earth's crust.

What can be concluded about the pre-flood world is that the continents we see today, along with the few submerged ones, are what the geography of the pre-flood world looked like.

The physical evidence uncovered proves this to be more of a fact than any other theory scientist claim. The evidence for the continents always being where they are now is overwhelming.

As for Antarctica, it probably was ice-free in the pre-flood world. It is possible that humans and animals lived there as depicted by many of the ancient maps. Or those maps simply depicted what the cartographers wanted the Antarctica to look like.

The change in that continent probably occurred after the poles shifted and the summers grew extremely cold. This enabled the ice to pile up to the thicknesses they are today.

There was no movement of the continents, just the fact that God allowed some of the Flood waters to remain for whatever purpose he had in mind. The key to all of this is we should not be worrying about what the pre-flood world really looked like as we will never get it back.

Instead, we should be learning the lessons God made by sending the flood. The flood is a warning to all post-flood people of what happens when one lives a life of disobedience to God's commands and instructions.

It is wise to learn from other people's mistakes, that way you can live a better life, one that is pleasing to God.

Works cited

#1. Editors, (2018), "Atlantis", History, https://www.history.com/topics/folklore/atlantis

#2.　　　　　　　https://www.papertrell.com/apps/preview/The-Handy-Mythology-Answer-Book/Handy%20Answer%20book/What-was-the-Egyptian-flood-myth/001137032/content/SC/52caff2a82fad14abfa5c2e0_Default.html

#3. Tee, D., (2024), "Understanding the Pre-Flood World", https://theoarch.wordpress.com/2024/08/13/understanding-the-pre-flood-world/

#4. Dismantling the Big Bang by Williams & Hartnett, pg 14 & 16

#5. Path of the Poles by Charles Hapgood

#6. Noah's Flood Did Take Place by Dr. Tee

Noah & the Pre-Flood World's Religions

Solomon explained it to us

In the modern world, new inventions may seem like no one has ever thought of them before. For example, the airplane and flight. Modern generations may only think that the Wright brothers were the first to contemplate flying like a bird.

But they were not. There are mythological accounts from Babylonian and Ancient Greece where flight is included. Even Leonardo da Vinci beat the Wright brothers when it came to considering flying (source #1).

What was missing from successfully achieving real flight in ancient times would be the technology needed to construct a legitimate and viable aircraft. However, religious beliefs do not suffer from the same obstacles.

Anyone at any time could, can, and did create their own religious belief systems. Solomon's words apply to this area of life as well. What is thought of today in the form of spirituality and supernatural beliefs was already thought of in the pre-flood world.

"9 What has been, it is what will be, And what has been done, it is what will be done. So there is nothing new under the sun. 10 Is there anything of which one might say, "See this, it is new"? It has already existed for ages Which were before us." (Ecc. 1)

Image by Coulet

The sacrificial system was in place

We do not know when God instructed Ada and Eve about the sacrificial system or what was involved. For some reason, God left that part out of the initial chapters of Genesis.

But we do read that Cain and Abel both practiced it at least once. Genesis 4 says:

"1 Now the man had relations with his wife Eve, and she conceived and gave birth to Cain, and she said, "I have obtained a male child with the help of the Lord." 2 And again, she gave birth to his brother Abel. Now Abel was a keeper of flocks, but Cain was a cultivator of the ground. 3 So it came about in the course of time that Cain brought an offering to the Lord from the fruit of the ground. 4 Abel, on his part also brought an offering, from the firstborn of his flock and their fat portions"

We also do not know how many of their brothers and sisters participated in the sacrificial system. However, later on, we read that at the birth of Enosh, son of Seth, men began to call upon the name of the Lord (Gen. 4:26).

So we do know that some sort of true religious belief was present in the pre-flood world. We also know this practice reached Noah's day. Enoch walked with God (5:21) and the following verses tell us that his faith and knowledge of God would reach to Noah.

Enoch lived long enough to know Lamech, Noah's father, thus this is the source for Noah's righteousness. Noah could not be righteous if he was not taught the ways of God and what God considered to be right or wrong.

True belief in God was prevalent in the pre-flood world. Since the NT tells us that God wants all men to be saved, (1 Tim. 2:3-4)he would not have left the pre-flood world without a witness to him and his ways.

"3 This is good and acceptable in the sight of God our Savior, 4 who wants all people to be saved and to come to the knowledge of the truth."

That witness is seen through Enosh to Enoch to Noah. Unfortunately, the people of the pre-flood world were vulnerable to the attacks of evil and were led away through temptation and other deceptive practices.

This falling away was so successful that only Noah and his family were left following what was right and true. This falling away led to the destruction of the pre-flood world.

The mysterious structures provide clues

While the pre-flood world had no knowledge of the future sacrifice of Jesus, the idea that cultic beliefs about Jesus are new is not true. Cultic beliefs may not contain the same elements in their belief systems but they remain false no matter what.

This means that we would not find any false religious beliefs like Arianism, and similar more modern false religions contain. But we would find false religions prospering in the pre-flood world.

If the descendants of Adam and Eve rejected what they taught about God, but wanted to stay religious then they would have constructed their own false beliefs related to what they were taught by both Adam and Eve.

To be deceptive enough to deceive their fellow citizens, then they would have included elements from the one true religion of that time. Just like it is done today where mystery religions and other false faiths include elements from the Bible to appear legitimate to the unwary.

When we look at the mysterious structures that are aligned to the solstices and the stars, we can conclude that some sort of sun worship was involved. Yes, these structures may have helped determine the changing systems, but that would not stop some people from creating a sun-god religion.

With the celestial alignments, it can be concluded that astrology was not the invention of the Babylonians. Instead, the knowledge to create this false belief could easily be found among the pre-flood world population. That is if their records had survived the flood.

The watchful heads of Easter Island could be another clue for another religious belief of the ancient pre-flood world. Those heads could be representations of the false gods, some members of that civilization worshiped.

This is as good a theory as any others that modern archaeologists have come up with. The Olmec heads may be a similar situation and some archaeologists have considered this possibility although the consensus is that the stone heads represent Olmec rulers (source #2).

This is something that can never be confirmed as all records for the builders of the mysterious sites and heads are lost. Plus, no neighboring country or society have any records on these structures and heads.

But since both ancient and modern civilizations created images for their gods, this act cannot be ruled out for the pre-flood world. Nothing is new under the sun and the pre-flood world would be first and they would be the original thinkers on religious practices.

Are there any other clues

Other than the practice of the pre-flood religious practices? The Bible does not provide any other clue than to say that all the people were evil. The definition of the term evil is quite long:

"#11. Having bad qualities of a natural kind; mischievous; having qualities which tend to injury, or to produce mischief

#2. Having bad qualities of a moral kind; wicked; corrupt; perverse; wrong;

#3. Unfortunate; unhappy; producing sorrow, distress, injury, or calamity

#4. Evil is natural or moral. Natural evil is anything which produces pain, distress, loss, or calamity, or which in any way disturbs the peace, impairs the happiness, or destroys the perfection of natural beings.

Moral evil is any deviation of a moral agent from the rules of conduct prescribed to him by God, or by legitimate human authority, or it is any violation of the plain principles of justice and rectitude. (#3)

So we can see that the evil the pre-flood world would include false religious beliefs. The second definition would certainly describe the essence or characteristics of false religions.

Their religious practices would exclude God and his ways while creating an attitude of rejection for Noah's preaching about the coming flood. Since they would not believe in God, they would also not believe that Noah's God would send a flood to kill them all.

We find this attitude in the modern age, as well as throughout the post-flood history of the world:

"3 Know this first of all, that in the last days, mockers will come with their mocking, following after their own lusts, 4 and saying, "Where is the promise of His coming? For ever since the fathers fell asleep, all things continue just as they were from the beginning of creation." (2 Peter 3)

As you can see from that verse, there is a slight clue about the beliefs and practices in the pre-flood world. The last line provides the clue. The pre-flood world was not different than the post-flood world.

This would include creating false religions and mocking Noah for his belief in God. Christians are mocked today for their belief in Jesus because scoffers refuse to accept the truth.

Conclusion

False religions would have been a part of the pre-flood world, for if they weren't, most likely, the population would not be as evil as God described in the Bible.

The term evil covers a lot of territory and is not limited to criminal behavior. It would include immoral behavior, perverted lifestyles and preferences, and much more.

Since the post-flood world has provided innumerable examples of unbelievers creating their own version of faith, with some based on the Bible or having biblical elements edited into their religious documents, it is not a stretch to say that this took place in the pre-flood world.

Gnosticism is just another example of the post-flood world members who create a faith after what they want to believe or highly prize. Mormonism is based largely on the Bible as are similar more modern religions have done.

To con people in the criminal world, the con men must have enough truth in their words in order to deceive others and get the money they are after. The same is true for false religions.

For evil to snare unsuspecting people, it must deceive humans into creating false religions holding just enough truth in their doctrinal statements and beliefs to trap unwary people.

It is interesting to note how many unbelieving scholars and archaeologists claim that the Biblical writers copied from false religions and secular myths. Yet, we find no real example of that taking place.

If the biblical authors copied, then it makes no sense for these other religions to copy from the Bible. They would know that the Bible would be false and their attempts to deceive others would fail.

The Bible is true even the flood account. That is why we have over 150 ancient secular flood stories. The Bible did not copy from any of them. The authors of those works had the information of the true flood passed down to them and they recorded what they had learned.

If the biblical flood was not true, then there is no reason for these ancient societies to record a flood story. There is no other ancient catastrophe that would spark all these different nations to write and accept these false flood accounts.

You do not get 150+ ancient nations recording a local flood at the same time in history and then memorializing those local floods into myths. The only account that makes sense is the Biblical one.

Works Cited

#1. A.W. (2024), "Ancient Aviators", Ancient-Wisdom, http://www.ancient-wisdom.com/flight.htm

#2. Minster, Christopher. (2024, June 25). The Colossal Heads of the Olmec. Retrieved from https://www.thoughtco.com/the-colossal-heads-of-the-olmec-2136318

#3. Webster, N. (re-published 2006). In Noah Webster's first edition of An American dictionary of the English language. Foundation for American Christian Education.

Noah & the Pre-Flood Technology

Introduction

Not much is known about the pre-flood world as all we have are clues as to how intelligent, creative, innovative, etc., they were. These clues do give us some insight to what was available material and tools wise plus, they provide an indication of the precise thinking the people had to work with.

The mysterious structures are just one of those clues that help us understand how sophisticated the thinking the people had in the pre-flood era. By piecing these clues together, one can realize how smart and capable the pre-flood population was.

Some question Noah's boat-building skills

The Bible only states that God told Noah to build the Ark. The same passage mentions the dimensions of the ark-

"15 This is how you shall make it: the length of the ark shall be three hundred cubits, its width fifty cubits, and its height thirty cubits. 16 You shall make a window for the ark, and finish it to a cubit from the top, and put the door of the ark on the side; you shall make it with lower, second, and third decks." (Gen. 6)

Skeptics point to the lack of information saying, "Where did Noah get his boat-building skills?" God is not going to put all the blueprint details or blow-by-blow construction steps in the Bible. That would be counter intuitive to what God is using the Bible for.

Plus, with all those details added, non-construction enthusiasts would read the Bible. Not just the book of Genesis but all of the Bible will be ignored because it would be too thick and interesting to only small individual groups of people.

We have to trust God's wisdom here as he would not entrust such a great and important project to just anyone. The first criterion that Noah would have to meet would be obedience.

God is not going to give the project to someone who would not obey his commands and instructions. Then we look at chapter 4 of Genesis and we see that Tubal-cain was a forger in all things metal.

The metal parts to help hold the ark together in rough seas were available to Noah. Because the Bible is the only source we have for the pre-flood world, we cannot say what Noah's exact boat-building experience was.

It is obvious that he and his sons had construction capabilities or the ark could not be completed as God wanted. The possibility that Noah and his sons hired help is a legitimate option.

However, all we know about the pre-flood Noah is that he was a righteous man. So it is impossible to say that Noah or his sons did not have boat-building skills.

We do not know what they knew or what they were taught. But the focus of the Bible is not about Noah and his sons abilities. That part of the Bible focus is on what happens when people disobey continuously and what God will do in this situation.

He punishes the disobedient and rewards the faithful. We have to go outside of the Bible to find more clues as to what technology the pre-flood world could have used and had available.

The massive stone heads

There are two examples that we can use to theorize about the pre-flood technology. The first are the Easter Island heads standing watch for something. We do not know what they are watching for but their presence, and the fact no one knows who built them or how they were built places them in the pre-flood construction era.

Then the second example would be the Olmec Heads. Archaeologists say an unknown civilization they have called the Olmecs carved these stone heads around 3000 years ago.

However, like the Easter Island heads, no one knows anything about the 'Olmec' heads. Yet their construction points to an artistry that is on another level than what Stone Age and copper tools could create.

The weight of the Easter Island heads reaches 87 tons approx., while the Olmec heads weigh roughly 40 tons. The weight alone puts these creations in the megalithic category as many of the stones used as a foundation for Baalbek, Stone Henge, and Malta 'temples' weigh the same as these heads (source).

Extant ancient documents do not record these structures nor list any tools capable of lifting or carving these stones. It is difficult to consider than primitive tribes could create these works.

If the Olmecs did exist, they would be primitive as no advanced material objects have been found for this group of people.

The work at Puma Punku

A different style of artwork is on display at this South American location. The complexity of the 'H' design puts the construction work out of reach of post-flood primitive people groups.

Like the Stone heads in the previous section, this artwork or construction project is only credited to the closest people to it. The intricate details require very sophisticated equipment, none of which survive or has been talked about by any people of the region.

What puts Pumapunku in the pre-flood category, despite what some archaeologists claim, is the fact that some of the stonework weigh up to 130 tons. Without contemporary ancient documentation and real verifiable evidence, then there is no way for ancient tribes to have constructed this site (Ibid).

On top of this, like many other mysterious structures and walls, the construction was so intricate that no mortar was needed. We do not find evidence of such skilled people in that era.

With the inability to identify the builders, this is another clue that the pre-flood world was able to develop, invent, and manufacture tools that are beyond the imagination of modern construction, etc., experts.

After all, America was able to develop from a primitive country into a super world power in less than 300 years. Just imagine what the people of that country could create if given at least another 700 years to develop tools, etc.

The possibility that the pre-flood world surpassed what the Americans did in their short existence is a legitimate possibility.

The multiple mysterious structures

The construction of mysterious structures, ones we know nothing about today, is another clue as to the type of technology the pre-flood world had. Their precise alignments, not only with placing stone upon stone several stories high but also with the solstices and stars provide more clues as to how the pre-flood world thought and worked.

What places these structures in the pre-flood category is not just the size and weight of the megalithic stones used in their construction, but also for the fact that all the builders disappeared.

Some of these structures, Gobekli Tepe, the Goseck Circle, Stonehenge, Ggantija, and more all have the same characteristics, details, and lack of information describing their construction, who built them, and why (source).

They also do not leave any plans, no neighboring countries have records of their construction, and there is no reason for the desertion of these sites. The only catastrophe that explains the lack of answers is Noah's flood.

It is not just the alignment that sets these structures apart from post-flood construction. In some cases, the acoustics are so perfect, that only master musicians and builders could construct or help construct some of these sites.

This tells us that the pre-flood world had access to fine tools and knowledge early post-flood people groups did not have.

The technology of the pre-flood world

Image by Pexels

From these and other clues that abound around the world, we get a fairly decent picture of the technology of the pre-flood world. That civilization's culture must have had a lot of people who were gifted inventors, manufacturers, designers, as well as construction people to achieve what they did.

They were able to invent and produce tools that could lift 40 to 130+ ton stones and place them with precision. Then they were able to carve so accurately that one, no mortar was ever needed, and the results were just about perfect.

On top of that with the forging skills of Tubal-Cain and whomever was taught by him, the metal pieces needed for those tools and other equipment were readily available.

While we cannot provide specifics for those tools and equipment, which must have been very sophisticated to locate the stars and align their buildings to them and the solstices, the clues point to the fact that the pre-flood world was very advanced.

We cannot not see their specific homes as those have mainly been destroyed but we can tell from the mysterious structures and other mysterious objects that the capability to create was supported by advanced tools.

So advanced that our post-flood eras could not duplicate them or even conceive of them. This was the type of technology and intelligence that was available in Noah and his sons, as well as available for them to use during their construction.

People question Noah's ability

This has been something that has taken place over the centuries. The reason people question Noah's abilities to build the ark with just his sons is because they believe unbelieving scientists, archaeologists, and historians.

These unbelieving people group have successfully convinced people that our ancestors were dumb, ignorant, afraid of fire, and incapable of doing more than hunting and surviving.

They have painted a bleak picture of our ancestors, stating they evolved and could not have the intelligence to achieve what we see with our own eyes. This false picture has distorted the truth about our past and led many to believe that Noah was incapable of building the ark and the Bible wrong.

As we search for and examine the clues, we get a different picture of our past. One that has two civilizations in it, with the first destroyed because they loved sin over God's righteousness, and the other heading in the same direction.

When one examines the evidence for the pre-flood world, we see that God gave the project to the most capable guy possible. Not only did he have the technology to help him build, he was an obedient person who did everything God had told him to do.

It is not a stretch to see that Noah and his sons had the ability to build an ark, the pre-flood world, including Noah and his family, was more advanced than our post-flood world.

If Archimedes could think of and invent different sophisticated weapons in his time, then it is not a stretch to see that the pre-flood world could develop the technology to build their structures, stone heads, and even boats.

While we do not know the length of Noah's cubit, we do know that he and his sons had the tools and knowledge necessary to complete the ark on time and without damage.

Conclusion

The Bible says, for God, nothing is impossible, which means that with God on Noah's side, building the ark is not some fanciful fairy tale. It is a true account of what took place in our past.

Noah & the Mass Extinctions

Was there more than one?

This is one of the bones of contention between Christians and scientists. The former believe and accept the fact that there was only one of these events in all of Earth's history.

The latter group claims that there are up to 5 mass extinctions that took place dating back millions and hundreds of millions of years.

Who is right? If you believe God, then the Bible is right and only one mass extinction occurred. But if you do not believe the Bible and take what science says over it, then a person may accept these 5 events as true.

There is an ongoing debate about this topic and which one is correct.

The 5 mass extinctions

The five events are dated as follows:

- Ordovician (444 million years ago; mya)

- Devonian (360 mya)

- End Permian (250 mya)

- End Triassic (200 mya) –

- End Cretaceous (65 mya) – the event that killed off the dinosaurs. (#1)

The problem with the data from these events is that they depend on the rocks and other dating factors taking place as scientists claim. So far, they have not proven the process or the length of time it took for those processes to work.

All scientists can do here is speculate because how would they tell the difference between one mass extinction and another? Scientists cannot see into the past nor can they view the extinctions as they happen.

All they can do is look at the remains and draw their conclusions. This is not observation in action but trying to decide what to do with all these remains, skeletons, and fossils.

No scientist knows how the remains got where they were or when the life forms actually lived. Fossilization does not come with a time scale and dating is their best guess. This is partly due to the fact that all scientific dating systems are founded on assumptions and unprovable data.

These mass extinction events are not the normal extinction rates that scientists claim take place ever million years or so. Their claim is that 10% of all species disappear every million years; then 30% every 10 million years; and 65% every 100 million years (Ibid).

But this is hard to believe that the evidence for these extinction rates and mass extinction rates lasted for this amount of time. It is a bit irrational and illogical to say that they did.

What separates the mass extinctions from these so-called normal extinction processes is that the former lose far more species than the latter no matter the time frame for the latter. The rate is set at 75%+ over a short time period, roughly 2 million years (Ibid).

Image by Siggy Nowak

The source for these mass extinctions

It is hard to see how scientists can gauge these rates given their placement in history. It would be miraculous to find physical evidence from so long ago and the evidence is attached to the remains and fossils arbitrarily so accuracy and correctness may never be part of the conclusion.

While scientists claim that there were 5 mass extinctions the physical evidence for the sources does not support that claim:

"Though the Cretaceous-Paleogene extinction is famous for being caused mainly by a huge asteroid, it's the exception. The single biggest driver of mass extinctions appears to be major changes in Earth's carbon cycle such as large igneous province eruptions, and huge volcanoes that flooded hundreds of thousands of square miles with lava.

These eruptions ejected massive amounts of heat-trapping gases such as carbon dioxide into the atmosphere, enabling runaway global warming and related effects such as ocean acidification and anoxia, a loss of dissolved oxygen in water." (#2)

The evidence the scientists point to describes exactly what took place during Noah's flood:

"Also, the 'fountains of the deep' were broken up. We can see this in that both the Atlantic and Pacific Oceans bear vast 'scars' or 'trenches' down the length of them as though the sea floor had erupted. As we are told.

Presumably, there was a layer of water beneath the earth's crust forming a 'cushion'. Without this cushion, we now see the effects of tectonic movement and we have earthquakes. Particularly the 'ring of fire' around the Pacific Ocean." (#3)

It is also possible that volcanoes did not make their appearance until after the flood. But we cannot be sure. This possibility does not relieve the scientists of the problem of how they can identify the source of the mass extinctions.

While volcanoes have been erupting for millennia, the actual evidence for earlier events should have been destroyed by the new destructive materials and eruptions.

There is no real way for scientists to tie the mass extinctions to those sources. They do not have any way to verify their claimed connections. Just like the meter that supposedly destroyed all the dinosaurs 65 million years ago. All scientists have is a deep crater-like impression to stake their claim to.

Even if meteorite rocks are found in that depression, those rocks do not connect the meteorite to destroying all the dinosaurs. It is all pure assumption and speculation.

Why is it expected that the depression would last for 65 million years? Wouldn't it be logical for it to have been filled in by now due to landslides, massive rains, and other natural disasters, that would have taken place in the region over those 65 million years?

The dinosaurs tell a different tale

It is often claimed that a meteorite caused the demise of almost all of the dinosaurs in the world. That is a mighty feat for one meteorite landing in the Central American region to accomplish.

"The Intermountain West is positively littered with dinosaur boneyards. In Late Jurassic rock layers from New Mexico to Montana, paleontologists have uncovered deposits that look like skeletal logjams." (#4)

These dinosaur deposits extend into the badlands of Drumheller, Alberta Canada. The nature of those bones does not indicate a meteorite source but more of a floodwater result:

"In the case of a sauropod nicknamed "Max," for example, nearly all the bones were found in a disarticulated pile." (Ibid)

However, there is nothing to connect the meteorite landing with the loss of dinosaurs. Again, scientists can only view the crater and the dinosaur deposits in the present. They have no way of looking into the past and seeing how the dinosaurs died off.

Scientists may have realized the weakness of their meteorite theory as they have now added super volcanic activity to their speculation about how the dinosaurs died. They also include a super tsunami in the mix (#5).

The descriptions given of the dinosaur deposits are very similar to what took place during the flood. The bones being buried under sediment would be consistent with biblical flood waters as would the volcanic eruptions on the other side of the globe in India (Ibid)

The scientists claim that those eruptions would have buried Alaska with enough volcanic material that reached the top of the highest modern skyscraper (Ibid).

Now if the volcanoes could do that, then it is possible for God to have enough water handy to submerge the tallest mountains. If one looks at this scenario honestly, there would not have to be that much water as the sediment, rocks, ash and other solid materials would elevate the water's surface and easily reach above the mountain tops.

It has been said that the dinosaur bones were left in a position that had the individual dinosaurs looking like they were running away from something that scared them.

This has not been proven as of yet but if it were so, a flood would scare the dinosaurs and make them run for what they thought was safety.

The evidence does not support multiple extinctions

This is just a brief look at what the evidence does tell us about the mass extinctions. There is just not enough to support 5 similar events. All the evidence does point to one catastrophe that was capable of delivering a global destruction that wiped out almost all the species living on Earth.

That catastrophe was Noah's flood. The reason this is so is because scientists do not have the ability to divide the remains and fossils into different epochs. Their theories and conclusions may sound like they can but in reality, they do not have any insight into what those remains exist.

They have not proven that the earth developed as they claim, nor have they observed that development. The same goes for the mass extinctions. They have not observed one of them yet feel they can extrapolate what they see into multiple catastrophic events.

The idea that physical evidence would survive for 1 million, let alone 441 million years is absurd. If so, these pieces of physical evidence must have been in protected areas free from the damage of myriads of natural and other disasters that took place over those time spans.

The physical evidence for the biblical flood is overwhelming. We see it almost everywhere we look. However, for the mass extinctions, the evidence must be twisted to fit the scientific theories as nothing connects the physical evidence with those claimed events.

This failure on the part of the scientists, or this willingness to ignore the actual source of the evidence, leads people away from the truth. The truth is that Noah's flood took place as the Bible said. The evidence supports it.

Works cited

#1. Hannah Ritchie (2022) - "There have been five mass extinctions in Earth's history" Published online at OurWorldInData.org. Retrieved from: https://ourworldindata.org/mass-extinctions

#2. Greshko, M., (2019), "What are mass extinctions, and what causes them?", National Geographic, Sept. 26, 2019, Retrieved from https://www.nationalgeographic.com/science/article/mass-extinction

#3. "What Exactly Were The FloodGates & "Springs of the Deep" In Genesis 7?", https://hermeneutics.stackexchange.com/questions/52582/what-exactly-were-the-floodgates-springs-of-the-deep-in-genesis-7

#4. Black, R., (2021), "New Process Helps Unscramble Dinosaur Boneyard Chaos", Sci Am, Retrieved from https://www.scientificamerican.com/article/new-process-helps-unscramble-dinosaur-boneyard-chaos/

#5. Summer, T., (2017), "Devastation detectives try to solve dinosaur disappearance", Science News, Retrieved from https://www.sciencenews.org/article/devastation-detectives-try-solve-dinosaur-disappearance

Understanding the pre-flood world

What Scientists say

Introduction

The Bible tells us of another world that existed before the modern one. These two worlds were divided by one giant cataclysmic event that altered our world's history as well as possibly altering the geography between the two worlds.

One of the clues that tip us off to this change is the lost continents scientists say existed at some point in time in the past. While their dating may be off, there may be some truth to their claims about these lost continents.

Some of these land masses may point researchers to the real geography of the pre-flood world. While there are roughly 6 main lost continents. Not all would contribute to the geography of the pre-flood world and remain evolutionary speculation that can never be verified.

Lost Continents with Indirect Influence

These are continents whose land masses have been extremely altered and do not exist today. Plus, their movement is dated to hundreds of millions of years ago which makes it hard to verify the claims made by geologists and other scientists.

#1. The Great Adria- said to have been demolished 240 years ago, this once great lost continent is described to be about the size of now Greenland. Its demise came about when it collided with now Southern Europe.

This collision is said to have peeled the top layer of Great Adria off and those remains helped form the Alps as well as many other mountain ranges dotting the Southern Europe topography.

Geologists also claim that leftovers from the Great Adria can be found on the surface in regions like the boot of Italy and Croatia.

#2. Argoland- This lost continent was playing a long-term game of hide-and-seek. It is said to have disappeared from view roughly 155 million years ago and only resurfaced in recent years.

Argoland is also described as once being a part of Australia yet bits and pieces of it are found in Southeast Asia. Also, it seems hard to imagine that a continent 3000 miles+ can be lost for so long.

Like The Great Adria continent, Argoland is said to have slipped underneath other land masses. It did not sink like Zealandia did but was crushed due to a collision.

In addition to that collision, geologists claim that Argoland broke up into the many islands that dot the ocean in the Southeast Asia region. This took place all the while parts of Argoland were migrating to different regions now occupied by Indonesia, Myanmar, and other Southeast nations.

While these two lost continents or their historical action cannot be verified, there may be a place for them in the construction of the new world that came to be after the flood.

We do not know or understand all of the turmoil that took place during the storms that dropped all the water or the volcanoes that erupted at this time. These may not be lost continents but what is being studied may be results of land mass alteration through the many violent behavior of those storms.

This physical alteration would come at any time during the 40 days of rain where the waters reached 15 cubits above the highest peak or the physical alteration could come as the waters receded.

Unfortunately, we are not given a detailed description of the flood's influence over the pre-flood world geography. We can only speculate as to what took place during those months when the waters rained down and remained on the earth.

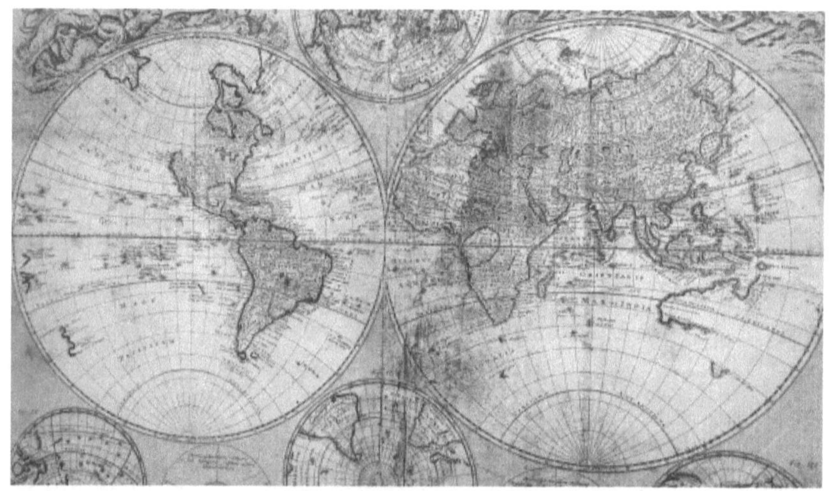

Image by francesco Foti

The supercontinents and the pre-flood world

Scientists and geologists have long lauded the theories that three supercontinents existed in our history. Like the contributions the previous two lost continents may have had on the pre-flood and post-flood geographies, these remain a possible geographical look of the pre-flood geography.

All the information for these three supercontinents comes from this link.

#1. Pannotia- this supercontinent is not the granddaddy of them all. It is said to have existed between 633 to 573 million years ago. However, there is still some skepticism whether this supercontinent actually existed or not.

Pannotia is supposed to have broken off from Rodinia which was the supercontinent prior to this one. During the life of this continent, volcanoes erupted creating the atmosphere that enabled the ice caps to develop.

These ice caps are speculated to have covered the entire planet. However, its lifespan was short in comparison to other supercontinents as it ceased to exist when Gandwana was born

#2. Gondwana- this supercontinent had a 400 million year lifespan giving it lots of time to develop life. It became a supercontinent when South America, Africa, India, Australia, and Antarctica, merged.

Gondwana's size has some scientists failing to categorize it as a supercontinent. It didn't even amass 75% of the total Earth's landmass. But despite its size, it is the supercontinent that existed at the time of the Cambrian Explosion.

Scientists also describe Gondwana as the first continent to create super-sized mountain ranges. These original mountain ranges were comparable to the Himalayan mountains and the erosion that took place over time, according to scientists, is what sparked the Cambrian explosion.

#3. Pangea- The name means all lands and scientists and geologists say that this final supercontinent contained all land masses on the Earth. Its lifespan ranged between 336 to 175 million years ago and its size only covered 1/3 the Earth's surface. The other 2/3 was all ocean.

Pangea was formed by the collision of minor continents Laurentia, Avalonia and Baltica collided together. Eventually, Pangea collided with Gondwana, This geographic phenomenon resulted in allowing the dinosaurs to come into existence after 96% of the life forms were killed in one of the great extinctions of 250 million years ago.

While it is difficult to accept these pre-flood or pre-history supercontinents, they do provide clues as to what the pre-flood world may have looked like before it was destroyed.

We also find clues that support the flood through volcanic activity, the great extinctions, and other clues. Since science cannot see into the past (Dismantling the Big Bang, pg. 16), it stands to reason that there was only one great extinction, divided up into different eras by those scientists who cannot accept the biblical account.

It is possible to think that Pangea may have been the geographic land mass the pre-flood world enjoyed until the Flood came. It makes some sense except for the length of time as well as the continental drift.

There is a much simpler explanation that is evident in the upcoming section.

The submerged lost continents

The following continents have been found existing under the water which provides some clue as to the extent of the pre-flood world geography. They are the ones that can be verified as well.

#1. Mu- This lost continent may have been born out of myth and legend, but myth and legend are often built upon actual events. What makes Mu stand out is the fact that humans lived on this land mass and were credited with technological knowledge and abilities.

Why researchers take Mu seriously is the myriad of submerged structures and other ruins found throughout the region Mu is said to have occupied. These structures are said to be megalithic in design and resemble the mysterious megalithic structures found on the surface around the world.

Its disappearance is said to be due to natural disasters or cataclysmic events that sunk the land mass except for a few mountain tops that were once mountains.

#2. Doggerland- Found on the other side of the world, Doggerland is the lost continent that connects Ireland and Great Britain to the rest of Europe. Its existence went unnoticed until some fisherman at the turn of the 20th century brought up animal tusks, Mesolithic and Neolithic tools, and fragments of human bones with their catch of the day.

So far only 43,000 square meters have been mapped giving researchers a fairly good idea of how life was lived on this lost continent. However, it was supposed to have been submerged by a tsunami which was the result of the underwater Storegga slides.

Ice melting and water level rising were two other contributors to creating this lost continent. Before this took place it is said that the inhabitants of this region lived near coastal areas or rivers and lakes. Doggerland is said to be above water until about 10,000 years ago.

#3. Zealandia- What remains of this lost continent are two islands that make up the country of New Zealand. Located off the coast of Western Australia, Zealandia covered 1.9 million square miles.

At one small point in the North Western region, Zealandia may have connected with a bit of Western Australia. This is a lost continent that is said to have existed 300 million years ago.

Zealandia is just one of the few lost continents that surround Australia, including the Louisiade Plateau. Just how they all fit together is a mystery.

The simple explanation for the existence of Zealandia, Doggerland, and Mu is Noah's flood. What their presence tells everyone is that when the flood waters receded not all the waters disappeared.

Some of the water stayed and changed the pre-flood geography to what we see today. This would explain why we find remnants of ancient townships, mysterious structures, and lost land masses underneath the water.

Even the speculated cataclysmic events are similar in nature to what we read took place in Noah's flood.

Conclusion

While people do not want to accept the existence of a global flood, a pre-flood world, or a change in geography, these lost continents provide more physical evidence for them.

The reason why they are evidence for Noah's flood is because scientists have not identified any other powerful destructive event that could cause this amount of destruction and change.

They can only speculate what took place in the past as they have no outside ancient manuscripts that provide a credible alternative. Most of the ancient documents like Plato's writings and the alleged writings about MU are mere legends embellished to satisfy an audience or make a grand point.

It is easy to accept Pangea as being part of the geography of the pre-flood world but the separation of the modern continents is probably due more to the flood waters not disappearing than they are due to continental drift.

Continental drift is mere speculation and there is no way to confirm the original locations of all the continents or that they moved in accordance with scientific theory.

Since we have more physical evidence supporting Noah's flood than any other biblical or scientific event, the biblical global flood account is true.

Works Cited

The Great Adria- Andrews, RG, (2019), "Lost continent revealed in new reconstruction of geologic history", National Geographic, https://www.nationalgeographic.com/science/article/lost-continent-revealed-by-plate-tectonics-model-greater-adria-mediterranean

Argoland- Young, O., (2023), "An Entire Continent Went Missing—But Scientists Have Found It Again", Atlas Obscura, https://www.atlasobscura.com/articles/lost-land-argoland

Super continents- Rails, E., (2024), "Supercontinents 101: Pannotia, Gondwana, and Pangea", Earth.com, https://www.earth.com/earthpedia-articles/supercontinents-101-pannotia-gondwana-and-pangea/

Mu- HTK, (2023), "Unraveling the Mystery of the Continent of Mu: A Lost Civilization", History to Know, https://historytoknow.com/continent-of-mu/

Doggerland- Moulton, M., (2020), "Doggerland: The Lost World Beneath the North Sea", History Guild, https://historyguild.org/doggerland-the-lost-world-beneath-the-north-sea/

Zealandia- Kruesi, L., (2024), "The lost continent of Zealandia has been mapped for the first time", National geographic, https://www.nationalgeographic.com/premium/article/the-lost-continent-of-zealandia-has-been-mapped-for-the-first-time

Image by Enrique

https://www.nationalgeographic.com/premium/article/the-lost-continent-of-zealandia-has-been-mapped-for-the-first-time

Noah & the Reason for the Flood

God does not lust for blood

Many critics of the biblical flood use a variety of arguments to say it never happened. They make inaccurate or false accusations against God and his personality.

These critics call him bloodthirsty, a maniacal murderer who lusts for blood, and so on. Yet, those arguments are not the reason why God sent the flood. Whether modern audience can accept the real reason or not remains to be seen.

These critics do not do their research and feel that their personal, subjective moral standards are superior to God's. This would be unfair to all people because the majority of the world's population never heard of those atheistic 'morals'.

How can they obey them if they do not know about them? At least God made sure his creation knew his rules. The punishment they got was in accordance with the 'crimes' they committed.

The flood was just punishment, not an act that fulfilled some sinful desire for blood.

There were moral people in the pre-flood world

The Bible tells us that Noah was a righteous man. That information comes in Genesis 6. However, if we read earlier chapters, we find that he was not the only righteous man in the pre-flood era. There were many before him.

In Genesis 4 we read these word- "26 To Seth also a son was born, and he named him Enosh. Then people began to call upon the name of the Lord."

There were people who sought after God and his ways. This had to be if Noah was going to get the instructions to be a righteous man. Without these earlier people, the teachings of God would have been long forgotten and not even reach Enoch.

Enoch was the 7th from Adam and the words of God had to have survived at least till that generation. We read in Genesis 5:22 that Enoch walked with God. Thus his knowledge and spirituality would have been passed down to Methuselah his son, Lamech his grandson and Noah his great-grandson

Noah missed meeting his great-grandfather by 69 years. But that was not long enough for Enoch's knowledge of God to disappear. It is possible that the spiritual decline started to take place during the time of Methuselah but we cannot be sure.

What we can be sure of is that at some point in Noah's life, the spiritual influence on life disappeared and all but Noah thought of evil all the time. Ezekiel 14 tells us that Noah's righteousness could only save himself.

We do not know the spiritual levels of his wife, sons, and their wives although Shem and Japheth may have been very spiritual before, during, and after yet not as righteous as Noah.

The scene is set as by the time God told Noah to build the ark, the world's population had devolved into a moral mess that excluded anything righteous or good. There was only one righteous man that we know of left in the world and God saved him and his family.

Image by Nino Souza Nino

The reason why the flood came

The New Testament tells us that 'men love darkness rather than light' and the pre-flood world has shown those words of Jesus to be very true. Like the post-flood world, the population of the pre-flood era saw that sin was more fun than being righteous or good.

"5 Then the Lord saw that the wickedness of mankind was great on the earth and that every intent of the thoughts of their hearts was only evil continually." (Gen. 6)

What may be confusing about their behavior is the term 'evil'. It sparks the imagination to think that all these people did was murder, rape, and abuse others.

However, when we look at God's definition of the term evil, and we should include the term 'wickedness' in there, we see a different story.

God defines evil and wickedness as disobedience to his commands and instructions.

Thus, the flood was sent as a punishment for their disobedience, not because God lusted after blood or desired to murder anyone. With this definition, we see a variety of 'minor' sins involved in the pre-flood people's actions.

Not only did they murder, rape, committed pedophilia, bestiality, and other heinous sins, these people also lied, stole, assaulted, cheated, committed adultery, had abortions, practiced LGBTQ preferences, gave and took bribes, and so on.

Keep in mind that Solomon told us in Ecc. 1 that nothing is new under the sun thus abortion and LGBTQ preferences were practiced throughout history including the pre-flood world.

What added to all of these sins and made them eligible for punishment is that none of these people repented of their sinful ways. They were all unrepented sinners.

The Old Testament blood sacrifices were in effect at this time as Cain and Abel practiced this act (Gen. 4). Thus an avenue for forgiveness existed for the pre-flood population to practice and receive forgiveness for their sins.

This is why the flood came. The people simply lived a life that was disobedient to God and his ways.

The depth of the depravity

Some people may think that it was unfair of God to include everyone in the punishment. We are not sure what happened to the newborns and babies up to a year or so old. God probably made provisions for that situation but we are not aware of them.

If he did make provisions and told everyone in the post-flood world about them, we may see an epidemic of newborns being killed carried on throughout history, so that they make it to heaven.

That is a minor issue that does not overshadow how depraved the pre-flood world became. Think about it. It was roughly 100 years between when Noah was told to build the ark and when he and his family entered it.

During all that time not one father came to Noah and his family and asked him to save his wife and family. Not one mother came to Noah and his family and asked them to save their babies and children.

Not one older brother or sister came to Noah and his family and asked them to save their younger siblings. Not one friend or relative did the same thing. Think about that. The pre-flood world was so depraved that they did not care about the survival of their loved ones or friends.

How do we know these requests did not take place? If they did and God or Noah denied the requests, the sons, or wives would have told their descendants and we would have ancient documents recording these denied requests.

We are not sure how the pre-flood world acted towards Noah and his family when they started to build the ark or during its construction period or even after it was completed.

They may have ignored the whole construction because they were so deceived they did not believe their society would be destroyed. After all, they had accomplished many great achievements in their short existence, which mysterious structures attest.

They must have thought that they were so great that nothing would touch or harm them. We cannot be sure because those reactions were not recorded and if they were, archaeologists have not uncovered them yet. Or they sit in Museums' storage rooms waiting to be translated.

The lesson to be learned

2 Peter 2 tells us of one more reason why God sent the flood- "5 and did not spare the ancient world, but protected Noah, a preacher of righteousness, with seven others, when He brought a flood upon the world of the ungodly; 6 and if He condemned the cities of Sodom and Gomorrah to destruction by reducing them to ashes, having made them an example of what is coming for the ungodly..."

The Bible tells everyone that God wants all men to be saved. Thus he used the Flood to warn his creation of what will happen if they follow the example of the pre-flood world.

God has provided a warning to encourage, motivate, and inspire, humans to make the right choices. No unbeliever can complain at the final judgment that their punishment for their unrepentant sinful lives is unjust.

They have been given 4000+ years of warnings of what happens to those who disobey God and refuse to repent of their sins. The flood is not an event that satisfies God's blood lust.

Instead, it is an event to prompt all of his creation to accept his plan of salvation and be saved like Noah and his family were.

Unfortunately, the lessons are ignored

As the Bible tells us, as it was in the days of Noah, so shall it be in the days when Jesus returns. Over the intervening 4000+ years, far too many people have ignored the warnings God has left.

They continue to prove the bible verse, 'man loves darkness, rather than light' true. Soon it will be too late to repent and the saddest person at the final judgment will be God.

He has the undesirable task of sentencing his creation to the lake of fire. That is not a happy event as his desire 'that all men be saved' is not fulfilled.

Image by Pexels

Noah & the Antarctica

The continent has been all ice

Every since its discovery in the 19th century, the world has known the Antarctica to be nothing but a wall of ice. That is the only look the post-flood world has seen of this continent... that we know of.

We cannot be sure if any of the ancient seafaring nations ever reached this cold land. The closest we know that any ancient nation has come to the Antarctica are the Romans.

Two Roman ships were discovered in 1982, in South America (#1). What they were doing there and was that their only destination or stop, we will never know.

If the Romans made it that far, then it is not out of the question that the Phoenicians or the Minoans could have sailed that far. What the continent looked like in ancient times is anyone's guess.

Image by Erika

What about the pre-flood world?

Despite what scientists say about moving continents, it stands to reason that Antarctica has always been in the same location. The flood waters did not move it or destroy the land mass.

The flood waters may have destroyed all the people on the continent as well as all the flora, fauna, and animals that were living there as well. But it is doubtful that it was filled with ice.

The pre-flood world seems to have had a different environment than the post-flood world. According to science, it was a very lush landscape filled with mountains, at least one river, and lots of plants, animals, and possibly humans (#2).

The scientific view has been that Antarctica has been under snow and ice for 34 to 35 million years approx. (#3) This dating seems far-fetched as there is no possible way for any scientist to verify that claim.

If the continent was ice-free at one time, the only logical time would be prior to the flood. This would mean that the pre-flood world civilization had an extra continent to expand to than the post-flood world.

A lush land would be an ideal location to move to if the neighbors on other continents were not to one's liking. We know that God gave the same command to Adam and Eve to multiply and fill the earth, just like he gave the command to Noah and his family.

Since it was a lush land, then the people had enough food to eat, water to drink, and plenty of space to spread out to raise their families.

What about the ancient maps?

Did these ancient maps depict a time in the post-flood world when the Antarctica was as lush as it was before the flood? This is hard to say since the maps giving this description pre-date the actual discovery of this continent.

The continent was discovered in the 19th century, yet those ancient maps come from hundreds of years earlier and are said to be based on more ancient maps. This is a mystery that has not been solved at this time.

The cartographers are said to be very accurate in their replication of the continent's coastline. This is a possibility if ancient post-flood sailors actually reached the continent's coastline.

What creates the mystery is the fact that those ancient maps place animal and plant life forms on the land mass. No one has seen either living on the continent for hundreds of years.

Who drew the ancient maps?

We do not know what paperwork Noah and his family took with them on the ark so it is possible that they had ancient maps at their disposal and it is probably that they didn't.

If they had maps from their time, then it is possible someone used them to copy from when they made other maps. Since there are no extant writings from Noah or his family, we will never know if they did or not.

Since ark landed somewhere in the Middle East, what need would Noah and his family have of these maps? Maybe they thought their descendants could use them to obey God's command to spread out and fill the earth but no confirmation is in sight.

It is puzzling that ancient map makers would accurately draw the coastline and place normal life forms as living on the continent. Some people have speculated that a very ancient civilization did live on Antarctica before it became ice and used some sort of aircraft to map their homeland.

It is possible as when the snows did not disappear and the plants and animals died out, if this is the case, then the people would have moved to other warmer continents bringing their maps, etc., with them.

But no one is sure anyone lived on the continent since the flood. Other people have contemplated that aliens mapped the area when they visited this planet. Of course, there is no verification or evidence suggesting this could ever have happened.

But because aliens are popular, many people accept this possibility. The only question is, how would ancient humans get a hold of those maps? Why would aliens map it in the first place?

It seems that with their spaceships, they could fly to any point on the globe and not need a map.

There is one theory about those ancient maps

This theory would take the mystery out of why those ancient maps showed Antarctica without ice and filled with life forms. It is possible that while reaching only the coastline and not traveling further inland, the map makers designed their maps to create Antarctica the way they wanted it to be.

In other words, they used their imaginations and wanted the Antarctica to be like their homelands. So they drew the flora and fauna and the animal life on their maps to give it a more friendly, homey feel to the continent.

That is the best theory that explains how those very old maps depicted a continent that has been filled with ice for a few thousand years.

Was the Antarctica a lost continent in the pre-flood world?

This is a very good question as we cannot be sure if the pre-flood population reached that land mass or not. Human remains have been found on the land mass but they date to only 175 years prior to their discovery in the 1980s (#4).

If other populations did live on the continent, then their tombs and graves are probably buried under the thick ice, unreachable today. Those bones are not evidence that anyone from the pre-flood world lived on the continent.

It could have been a lost continent to that human population like it was for thousands of years after the flood. It is doubtful it was lost but like most aspects of the pre-flood world, we will never know the correct answer.

All information about the pre-flood world has been destroyed in the flood and we are only left with clues to use to guess.

The continent was never lost

There is a lesson to be learned here, even though we cannot be sure what Noah and his family knew about Antarctica. The land mass did not suddenly develop out of nothing or from the flood waters.

As it is known that some of the water did not disappear from the earth, it could not have created the landmass. This topic just adds to the mystery of the pre-flood world except [t for one important fact.

The continent has never been lost. God knew where it was all the time. Whether humans were courageous enough to explore the ancient world and discover this land earlier than it was, is something we will never know.

But the fact that God knew where it was, brings people a bit of peace of mind. No matter how alone you may feel or how secluded you are, God knows where you are. You are not lost, undiscovered, or alone.

Humans can take comfort in that fact. To get in contact with Jesus, and get his companionship, one just has to believe in him and accept him as their savior. That is a comforting thought. When humans reject or do not want you, God is there to fill the void letting you know you are loved and wanted.

———

Works cited

#1. Pellegrino, C., (1991), 'Unearthing Atlantis, Vintage Books, pg. 110.

#2. Schultz, C., (2013), "Here's What Antarctica Looks Like Under All The Ice"", Smithsonian, https://www.smithsonianmag.com/smart-news/heres-what-antarctica-looks-like-under-all-the-ice-92354118/

#3. Oskin, B., (2013), "What Antarctica Looked Like Before the Ice", Live Science, https://www.livescience.com/27715-antarctica-before-ice.html

#4. Henriques, M, (2020), "A frozen graveyard: The sad tales of Antarctica's deaths", BBC, https://www.bbc.com/future/article/20180913-a-frozen-graveyard-the-sad-tales-of-antarcticas-deaths

Why Noah's Ark Will Not Be Found

People want evidence

This is what the modern world has turned into. Due to the rise in scientific influence and its demand for physical evidence, every day people want to see evidence before they accept a premise as true.

The demand for evidence has overwhelmed the population elbowing the requirement for faith to the sidelines. It used to be that people believed the Bible without the need of any evidence.

That is not blind faith but acknowledging the fact that without faith one cannot please God. Also, it is an act of obedience as faith has always been the requirement for salvation and other biblical topics.

However, when science was placed as an authority the demand for real physical evidence rose and people stopped obeying God and wanted to see more and more physical evidence.

In response to this demand, many Christians and other explorers got the idea to search for Noah's ark. They felt that if the story was true and to convince everyone that it was true, discovering the ark was a necessity.

Different organizations have spent millions searching for the ark, as well as spending hours held in police custody during their searches. Needless to say, their efforts did not produce the ark.

All they produced was geographical land sites and other artifacts that were and are easily refuted.Nothing ties those discoveries to the real ark as no one really knows where the ark landed in the first place.

Image by Makalu

The ark landing

This is one of the more controversial aspects of the search for Noah's ark. Some readers of the Bible have confused the text's language:

"4 Then in the seventh month, on the seventeenth day of the month, the ark rested upon the mountains of Ararat" (Gen. 9).

For some reason, they ignored the words 'mountains of' and focused on the term Ararat instead. Many explorers hiked the sides of this mountain in search of the ark (1).

They didn't find anything except geographical formations which they took to be the ark after 3000 years approx. Other explorers and researchers did not ignore those words 'mountains of' and said the ark rested 176 miles away from Mt. Ararat (2).

Still more people went to the Zargo Mountains of Iraq to find the ark (3). There have been countless searches for Noah's ark through the centuries with many people claiming more than these three locations to be the landing area of the ark.

This is one compelling reason why Noah's ark will not be found. No one knows exactly where the mountains of Ararat are located. There was an ancient nation called Ararat which some claim the spelling came from the ancient kingdom called Urartu

"Ancient Armenia, located in the south Caucasus area of Eurasia, was settled in the Neolithic era but its first recorded state proper was the kingdom of Urartu from the 9th century BCE." (4)

But as one can see, Urartu did not exist at the time of Moses writing about the flood. A case may be made that it was but that is a topic for another day. The historical confusion is another compelling reason why the ark will never be found.

Reasons why the ark will not be found

Besides the two reasons already listed, there are other reasons why the ark would not have lasted for 3000 years. If you read the flood account you will find that Noah was to cover the ark in pitch, both inside and out.

"14 Make for yourself an ark of gopher wood; you shall make the ark with compartments, and cover it inside and out with pitch." (Gen. 6)

Pitch, or oil, is not a preservative. It is a waterproofing material but nothing that will make the gopher wood last for thousands of years. The wood would have rotted by this time and probably did so before the time of Babel. Give or take a hundred years.

Another reason the ark will not be found is that where were Noah and his family going to stay once the flood waters were gone? Some people have suggested that Noah and his sons would have dismantled the ark to build new homes but that may have been a wasted effort (5).

It would have been just as easy for them to use the ark as their initial home until the world was populated with mature trees again. It is hard to say as there are no extant records describing what took place immediately after the flood.

All the Bible tells us is that Noah planted a vineyard and we have no idea what the sons did once the flood ended. The Bible also said he began farming, which makes sense as he and his family needed food (Gen. 9).

Either way, if they lived in the ark in those early years or dismantled it, the wood would not last for thousands of years. Any petrified wood could not be identified as ark wood because no one would know what gopher wood looks like or is.

To be petrified the wood would have to be quickly buried under mud, silt, or volcanic ash and then lay in that buried state for a long time. Scientists say that length of time is millions of years but that is mere speculation (6).

Here is the key as to why any petrified wood discovered in any of the regions claimed to be the ark's landing site. The petrified wood is not wood but the minerals that replaced the rotting wood (Ibid).

Any examination of petrified wood pieces would not discover gopher wood but those minerals that replaced it. Thus no one can rely on petrified wood as evidence for the ark's final resting place.

One big reason why the ark won't be found

It is the same reason why we cannot find the real Mt. Sinai or the location of the Garden of Eden. As proven by the example of the traditional Mount Sinai, next to St. Catherine's monastery, people would worship the ark and deify it.

Their attention and reverence would go to the ark and not to God. Like the burial of Jesus, people worship that location and claim it is holy when it is not. That is an insult to God.

Besides that, we do not need to discover the ark or its final resting place. Noah's flood is the one biblical event that has the most physical evidence proving it true (7).

There is no hope of proving any artifacts discovered in any of those locations as being associated with the ark or Noah. We do not need them with all the other evidence like sunken coastlines, villages, mysterious structures, bones of animals and humans in caves and fissures found around the world and much more (Ibid).

This includes trying to tie any remnants of the ark to 'the' ark. There is no way to make the connection and skeptics would have a field day refuting any claims.

Image by Bereswchit

It takes faith

While we have so much evidence for Noah's flood, it still takes faith to believe the biblical record. We do not know how Noah and his sons built such a large ship, how they weathered the storm, and much more. Everything about the flood has to be taken by faith.

Except for the lesson that God provided through this biblical event. Instead of searching for the ark, people should be learning what disobedience is going to cost them.

Romans 6:23 reiterate what God taught us with the biblical flood account:

" For the wages of sin is death, but the gracious gift of God is eternal life in Christ Jesus our Lord."

Both are warnings that need to be taken seriously.

Works cited

#1. NEW, (2024), "Mount Ararat" New World Encyclopedia, https://www.newworldencyclopedia.org/entry/Mount_Ararat

#2. Johnson, RB, (2021), "Evidence that Noah's Ark Landed on a Mountain 17 Miles South of Ararat", Ancient Origins, https://www.ancient-origins.net/human-origins-religions/noahs-ark-south-ararat-009725

#3. Op Cit https://www.newworldencyclopedia.org/entry/Mount_Ararat

#4. Cartwright, M., (2018), " Ancient Armenia", World History Encyclopedia, https://www.worldhistory.org/armenia/

#5. Blakemore, E, (2022), "Why Noah's Ark will never be found", National Geographic, https://www.nationalgeographic.com/magazine/article/noahs-ark-archaeology-search-science

#6. Phelan, J., (2022), "How long does it take to make petrified wood?", Live Science, https://www.livescience.com/32316-how-long-does-it-take-to-make-petrified-wood.html

#7. Noah's Flood Did Take Place: Analyzing the Non-Scientific Evidence by Dr. David Tee.

Conclusion

The pre-flood world is an enigma

There is no other way to describe that era. Because the world of that time was destroyed in Noah's flood we do not have any valuable information to analyze their lives and civilizations.

It would be interesting to know if that period had different nations speaking different languages. The post-flood civilization had one language because Noah and his family spoke only one.

It would also be interesting to read about their daily lives prior to everyone committing sin and thinking of evil all the time. What they did for fun and entertainment, what sports they played, and if they were able to create transportation as we know it today.

Given the fact that metalwork existed at that time, it would be interesting to see what tools they invented as well. The mysterious structures that permeate the world today only tease us concerning the technology that the world could have invented.

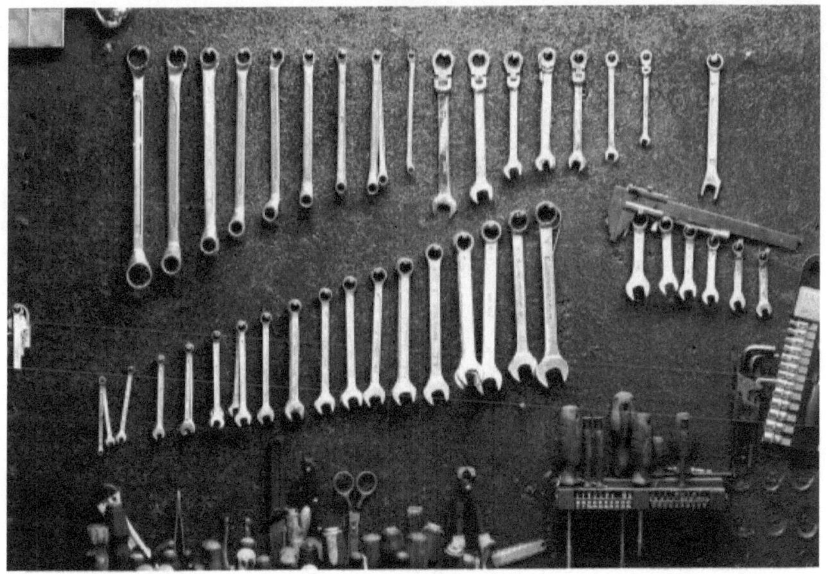

Image by Raduslaw Kulupa

These are all questions of wonderment as we only receive a few clues from the Bible, archaeology, and science. Those clues only provide a tidbit of information about what went on in the pre-flood world.

Looking at the pre-flood world through the varios clues is like what Paul said. We look through a glass darkly. In other words, we do not see the full picture of the pre-flood world. Given the clues we can only conclude that the pre-flood world was exactly like our world.

It is highly doubtful that the geography was anything like scientists have described. The presence of the sunken lost continents tells us that no land mass moved anywhere at any time.

The concept of super continents being able to separate themselves has no foundation and is based solely on the looks of each continent. In other words, the concept of land masses being joined together to form one continent is read into those shapes.

There is no real physical evidence or observation to support those claims. It would also have to be a massive and powerful natural disaster to provide the energy for those landmasses to move even one inch.

Judging from the many mysterious structures found around the globe, the pre-flood world did one better than the initial post-flood civilization. The people of that era obeyed God's command to reproduce and fill the earth.

We find physical evidence everywhere showing that they were initially obedient to God. Who knows, maybe some of the people in the pre-flood world moved away early from those who were following the path of Cain and formed their nations of their own.

Over the years, they two slowly degraded into a sin-loving people. It is something to speculate about as many people move away from troubled areas to find peace, quiet, and safety for their families.

As for technology, the experts have said that the mysterious remains were constructed using tools and technology that are almost or are beyond the level of what we have in the modern world.

It is reasonable to accept the fact that we cannot find any evidence of those tools because they were made of metal and other raw materials that easily decayed over time.

By the time of the Diaspora of Babel, any remaining objects from the destruction of Noah's flood may have deteriorated and disappeared by the time the new people groups reached their new homes.

It is fun to speculate about a world we will never know. There are so many possibilities that could have taken place that we have no idea what that civilization accomplished. Save for the mysterious structures and other objects archaeologists find from time to time.

But there are a few lessons that the modern world can learn from the first civilization. The first lesson is obvious and taught by preachers and Christian professors throughout the history of the post-flood era.

That obvious lesson is that sin does not lead to paradise but to destruction. That is what Peter told us in his second epistle. The remains of the pre-flood world and the flood accounts serve as a warning to everyone who wants to do evil and disobey God.

It is a mighty important lesson which is why over 100 flood accounts still exist. Another lesson that can be learned from the pre-flood world is that whatever we thought of since the flood ended, they thought of as well.

There may not have been planes, trains, cars, or trucks, but they thought of transporting themselves in some way. Who knows, maybe there were those items. We will never know.

There is another important lesson to be learned form all of this information. People may have trouble identifying with Christ and his example of how to live. That is due partly to his being God as well as human.

But Noah was fully human and he provided the example that it is possible to be righteous, make the right decisions, in a very dark world. He also showed that one can keep one's family safe in a similar situation.

When we look at them, we see ourselves. In today's world, we have people who are holy, righteous, and want a peaceful, crime-free society. We also have those who disobey God and only think of evil all the time.

That lesson should motivate Christians to re-energize and re-power their efforts to win as many souls as possible, as well as teach them Christ's commands.

That is what Jesus said in the Matthew's Great Commission. We should not lose hope but continue to let Jesus work through us. It is time to put away pursuing what the world has to offer and get serious about fulfilling Jesus' commands.

It is not a pretty site to see one's reflection in this type of mirror. We know that sin will never win but why let it claim more victims than those that get to go to heaven?

Let's use the example of the pre-flood world to motivate and inspire our evangelical, apologetic, and educational efforts. With God's might and power, we can be more successful than ever.

We just need to accept the truth and follow the Bible correctly to hear those words 'well done, thou good and faithful servant'.

Addendum
Noah & the Voice of God

The inner conviction

This seems to be God's choice of communication with his followers in the post-flood world. Throughout Biblical history we do see God interacting with specific people but generally he did not talk to them directly.

More often than not, God spoke to his prophets who then relayed God's message to the people. We see this taking place with Samuel, Nathan, Jonah and other prophets.

These men knew God's voice and had no doubt or confusion they were speaking with God. Unfortunately, the Bible does not always give us clues to recognize God's voice.

When he spoke to Elijah, it was a still small voice and most likely there was a similar voice when he spoke to his prophets. There was no sense in overwhelming his prophets with a thunderous voice.

One reason why God did not need to speak directly to his people in the post-flood world is that he had left a body of information, including the Bible, where his will was clearly laid out.

Sometimes, God used circumstances to help his people understand what he wanted them to do (1).

What about the pre-flood world

This is more of a mystery as we are not told what written instructions God gave his people. We can conclude that he made his will known through a variety of means as both Cain and Able knew they had to make a sacrifice to God at the right time.

However, the Bible does tell us that God spoke directly to Adam, Eve,m the Serpent, Cain, and Noah. We can include Enoch in that list as the early chapters of Genesis tell us that he walked with God.

The interesting part about Eve is that she knew the difference between the serpent's voice and God's. her words were "2 The woman said to the serpent, "From the fruit of the trees of the garden we may eat; 3 but from the fruit of the tree which is in the middle of the garden, God has said, 'You shall not eat from it or touch it, or you will die." (Gen. 3)

She knew that she was not talking to God thus there is a distinct difference between God's voice and every other voice in the world. If one looks at Jacob's encounter with an angel (Gen. 31) Jacob knew the difference between the angel's voice and God's.

These different occurrences tell us that when Noah heard the instructions from God, he knew he was not being fooled. He could tell who was speaking to him.

"13 Then God said to Noah, "The end of humanity has come before Me; for the earth is filled with violence because of people; and behold, I am about to destroy them with the earth...22 So Noah did these things; according to everything that God had commanded him, so he did." (Gen. 6)

Because Noah knew who he was talking to, he did not talk back, complain, or make excuses. He got all the instructions and his family, then set out to obey everything God had told him to do.

Some additional words

We do not see any difference between then and now. God;'s voice will be distinct from every other voice in the universe But we have to be careful.

God does not directly talk to people that much anymore and many people have been led astray to false missions or Christian work. One has to be discerning and make sure they are hearing God's voice, call, or inner conviction.

The voice we hear has to be in line with what Scripture teaches us. God does not lead his people to sin or disobey his word. There is a very good reason why God wrote the Bible.

That was done so that God's creation could hear God's voice clearly. The key is to make sure one is actually hearing God's voice.

Works Cited

#1. BGEA (2010), "Answers", Billy Graham Evanbgelistic Association, https://billygraham.org/answer/in-biblical-times-did-god-speak-to-people-in-a-voice-they-could-hear/

Addendum 2
Noah's Influence on the post-flood world

The Bible tells us that Noah lived 350 years after the flood took place. That fact may not let people comprehend the the amount of time Noah spent on this earth after the flood.

Shem, as the Bible records, was 98 years old when the flood took place. After the flood he was 100 when his son Arpachshad was born. Between Arpachshad birth and Abraham's, the length of time was 292 years.

Take away 292 from 350 and you end up with 68 years. This means that Noah was still alive until Abram or Abraham was 68 years old. With this chronology you can see that the righteous Noah could have had a lot of influence on the post-flood world.

If he did not, then his son Shem lived for another 500 years after the flood giving the world access to his experiences, wisdom and knowledge. What this also means is that both Shem and Noah experienced babel in some form.

We cannot be sure exactly what they experienced as the Bible stops talking about these two gentlemen once Abram's birth is announced. It is possible that Noah and Shem taught their descendants what God told Noah right after the flood:

"Then God blessed Noah and his sons, and said to them, "Be fruitful and multiply, and fill the earth" (Gen. 9:1) but as we read further in the book, their descendants did not want to do that.

Instead, they wanted to remain together and build a great name for themselves.

"Now all the earth used the same language and the same words. 2 And it came about, as they journeyed east, that they found a plain in the land of Shinar and settled there. 3 Then they said to one another, "Come, let's make bricks and fire them thoroughly." And they used brick for stone, and they used tar for mortar. 4 And they said, "Come, let's build ourselves a city, and a tower whose top will reach into heaven, and let's make a name for ourselves; otherwise we will be scattered abroad over the face of all the earth." (Gen 11).

It is possible that the people wanted to escape Noah's and Shem's instruction and influence thus they traveled to find a new home. We cannot be sure of what exactly took place to cause them to search for a new area to live.

They may have found the area where the ark landed was too small for them and needed a larger area to set up a kingdom. God does not provide the reason for their travels.

However, Noah's and Shem's longevity after the flood provides a clue as to why Abram was a righteous man. Their influence could easily have reach Abram through various ways including the men born between him and Shem.

The fact remains though, that both Noah and Shem could have had a lot of influence on the people before and after Babel. The people's arrogance and rebellious nature is not surprising.

For even in Jesus' time, people did not accept his words nor followed him in spite of all the miracles he performed. Since people have free choice, Noah's and Shem's influence would only go as far as those who accepted their words and guidance.

We do not know if all the people thought like the leaders of the pre-Babel civilization, but their refusal to leave the area and found new areas brought the same punishment.

Some of them may have seen the error of their ways, repented and followed Noah's and Shem's teachings. Which wold also explain why Abram was worthy to be called of God.

The pre-flood world and the pre-Babel era will always remain a mystery to those in the modern world. The clues only give us a little insight to what may have taken place.

But one thing is for sure, Noah had some influence before he died.

Books by the author

———

Noah's Flood Did take Place: An examination of the Non-Scientific Evidence

Archaeology & the Believer

The Church and Science: Get All the facts

Archaeology:What you Need to Know

God, Korea, & Me

The Future of Biblical Archaeology

Freelance Writing For Money: A Guide to the Freelance Writing World

RV Life: A New Way to Live

About the Author

Dr. David Tee has spent the last few decades studying the Bible, History, and archaeology. He has earned degrees in all three fields and now puts what he has learned into this work. Over the years he has written other excellent books that help Christians strengthen their faith. Other work can be found at his websites and Medium channel.

Read more at https://theoarch.wordpress.com/.

www.ingramcontent.com/pod-product-compliance
Lightning Source LLC
Chambersburg PA
CBHW031420150726

47989CB00002B/729